Questioning Crime and Criminology

D0218014

Questioning Crime and Criminology

edited by

Moira Peelo and Keith Soothill

WILLAN
PUBLISHING

Published by

Willan Publishing
Culmcott House
Mill Street, Uffculme
Cullompton, Devon
EX15 3AT, UK
Tel: +44(0)1884 840337
Fax: +44(0)1884 840251
e-mail: info@willanpublishing.co.uk

Published simultaneously in the USA and Canada by

Willan Publishing
c/o ISBS, 920 NE 58th Ave, Suite 300
Portland, Oregon 97213-3644, USA
Tel: +001(0)503 287 3093
Fax: +001(0)503 280 8832
e-mail: info@isbs.com
website: www.isbs.com

First published 2005

ISBN 1-84392-126-X paperback
     1-84392-127-8 hardback

British Library Cataloguing-in-Publication Data

A catalogue record for this book is available from the British Library

Project management by Deer Park Productions, Tavistock, Devon
Typeset by GCS, Leighton Buzzard, Beds
Printed and bound by T.J. International, Padstow, Cornwall

Contents

Notes on the contributors

Brian Francis is Professor of Social Statistics and Director of the Centre for Applied Statistics, Lancaster University. He researches into quantitative criminology, particularly criminal careers, and is interested in the application of new statistical modelling ideas to criminological datasets to improve understanding of crime. Currently he directs one of the regional UK ESRC National Centre for Research Methods nodes.

Chris Grover is a Lecturer, Department of Applied Social Science, Lancaster University. He has published widely on income maintenance and labour market policy. His focus is upon the ways in which the moves to more authoritarian benefit regimes and the shift to subsidising low paid employment can be understood as reconstructing the reserve army of labour to manage a range of social and economic dilemmas.

Simon Holdaway is Head of the School of Law, Professor of Criminology and Sociology and Co-Director of Centre for Criminological Research, The University of Sheffield. A former police officer and mature student at Lancaster University, he has published widely about many aspects of criminology. His specialism is the police, in particular the occupational culture of policing and race relations within constabularies. His latest research project was a two year study of Black Police Associations. Full details of his publications can be found at http://www.shef.ac.uk/law/staffd/holdaway/research.htm.

David Lyon is Director of the Surveillance Project and Professor of Sociology, Queen's University, Kingston, Ontario, Canada (www.queensu.ca/sociology/Faculty/Lyon.htm). While his current work is all in Surveillance Studies and most recent books are *Surveillance after September 11* (2003) and *Surveillance as Social Sorting: Privacy, Risk and Digital Discrimination* (ed., 2003) he also has research interests in Networked Technologies, Postmodernity and the Sociology of Religion.

Fiona Measham is a Senior Lecturer in the Department of Applied Social Science, Lancaster University. She has conducted research in the field of alcohol and illicit drug use, gender, licensed leisure and cultural criminology for over 15 years. Recent research includes a study of 'binge drinking' and bounded consumption; an analysis of gambling and state regulation of leisure; an historical analysis of the attempted criminalisation of barmaids and an exploration of trends in drug use, pharmacological pleasure and the emergent criminology of transgression.

Moira Peelo is Senior Honorary Research Fellow, Department of Applied Social Science, Lancaster University. Her research career has focused on aspects of marginality in education, health and crime. Her criminology research has included projects on poverty and crime, young offenders, offenders as victims of crime and newspaper representations of homicide.

Mike Presdee is Director of Criminology at the University of Kent. He has written widely on the connections between culture and crime and the new field of Cultural Criminology. He is the author of *Cultural Criminology and the Carnival of Crime* (Routledge, 2000) and co-editor of *Cultural Criminology Unleashed* (Glasshouse Books, 2004).

Keith Soothill is Professor of Social Research, Department of Applied Science, Lancaster University. His research interests are in the areas of homicide, sex offending, criminal careers and crime and the media. He has taught criminology for over 30 years with over 150 publications, including the co-authored book, *Making Sense of Criminology* (Cambridge: Polity Press, 2002). He is currently Chair of the Department of Health's National Programme on Forensic Mental Health R&D.

Introduction

Crime is exciting but what of criminology?

Moira Peelo and Keith Soothill

Crime is exciting. As a society, we have a fascination with the darker side of life. Television and film are awash with cops and robbers, murders and detectives, along with the unravelling of secrets in our midst. Robbery, prisons, courts, judges, police stations are all the stuff of television drama and serials. Oxford and Glasgow are regularly saved from tidal waves of murder only by especially gifted and insightful detectives, while in the blighted Midsomer villages, devious criminals are detected deviously.

Criminology, by comparison, appears as a relatively dull subject in which data and theory are used to unpick all that people of 'common sense' know to be obvious truths about the state of crime in Britain and America today. Current 'common sense' says that crime is on the increase, society is more out of control than ever before, courts do not punish offenders severely enough and that 'prison works'. For many, 'right' and 'wrong' are perceived as obvious and a matter of rational choice; for some, offenders are seen as different to the rest of society. Others view poverty as a direct cause of crime, while for another group, crime is a matter of socially agreed rules. Everyone's 'common sense' is passionately held and self-evident.

Students quickly learn that criminology is a strange world. In fact, criminology embraces several different worlds. There is the academic world that criminology occupies just like any other academic discipline. But it also embraces a more public world that is much more controversial. Yet, as criminology has grown massively over recent years as a favoured undergraduate subject, it seems to have lost much of its impact in the public arena. Unlike in the 1960s when criminologists wrote newspaper columns in national newspapers, criminologists are nowadays much more restricted to 'guest appearances' as experts on rather specific topics. This is curious at a time when 'law and order' concerns are placed at the very top of electoral issues that governments and oppositions think will excite the interest of the voting population. The task of the criminological enterprise is to explore and explain crime and yet criminology appears to have been largely sidelined in the public arena.

This is, in part, related to the ways in which the reality surrounding crime phenomena often turn out to be quite different once the data is explored in depth. Long-held beliefs come under pressure. To make matters worse, the data take some unpicking. Analysis in criminology is complicated, often statistical and can – on occasions – appear so analytical as to have little to do with daily life. Further, the actuality of 'crime' is, while distressing, more mundane: theft, violence, illegal killing is often much less dramatic than the extraordinary cases that make headlines or the basis for TV drama.

Criminology, sadly, is not designed to entertain, at least not in the same way as crime drama. It is, like all academic study, intended to be a systematic framework for analysis of its main focus – in this case, crime and criminality. Central to the study of crime is a concern with knowledge: with how we 'know' about crime, with where the information comes from and with detailed evaluation of the meanings of that knowledge. Crime as a consumer product, crime as a real-life event and crime as a subject of study are not all always the same phenomenon.

Further, every academic discipline has controversies and conflicts that often appear to students to cloud the core issues. However, dispute, disagreement and conflict are the fuel that drives any discipline forward. In applied social science studies, disciplines emerge, evolve and develop through conflict; and often, rather than having clearly demarcated boundaries, 'disciplines' turn out to be groups of academics with shared interests who are in a permanent state of discussion over the supposed limits of their studies. Our last book focused on trying to make sense of criminology (Soothill, Peelo and Taylor, 2002) and, following David Garland (2002), we see criminology as developing a specific kind of discourse about crime. We would argue that it is a disputed discourse, and that understanding the disputes and their origins helps students of criminology to make sense of crime and criminality, as well as to make sense of criminology, in the present day.

As an applied social science discipline that has evolved, borrowed from related subjects and re-formed, criminology has also responded to dynamic changes within society over time. New social issues take on greater or lesser importance at different points in time, and old answers fade in the face of new questions. Hence, given that criminology has its own history of theoretical development, understanding changes both within the discipline and within the social context for criminological studies helps us to make sense of crime and criminality.

So, in this book, some of the key themes discussed relate to social history and to the history of criminology, to evaluating knowledge about crime and to testing the current boundaries of criminology. Questions that we set out to explore included:

- What is crime: how is it defined in populist politics and what, currently, constitutes 'common sense'?
- History of crime and criminology: why does it matter? How does the present echo the past?
- Criminology: what makes academic knowledge different to other types of knowledge?
- Criminology: what are the boundaries of criminology? Is it becoming too narrow or too wide in its interests as an academic discipline?
- The future of criminology: what is the way forward?

None of the chapters will contain all these themes, but all the chapters will contain some of them. When understood as developing and dynamic, in relation to a changing social context, then criminology recovers some excitement. It is certainly different to other studies and, potentially, adds greatly to understanding society and its members. This book attempts to take you beyond the introductory level and to confront themes and questions that are crucial to developing a deeper understanding of crime and criminology.

In Chapter 1, Keith Soothill argues that general theories of crime emerge within the context of their own times. He shows us the contribution and limitations of general theories, while also illustrating their role in generating conflict and disagreement – thus providing dynamic momentum to the development of the distinct discourse of criminology. Soothill focuses on the development of criminology through four key theoreticians rather than offering an exhaustive history of criminological theory. The four chosen are: Cesare Lombroso, Edwin Hardin Sutherland, Robert King Merton and Travis Hirschi. Each can be seen as having produced a 'general theory' that attempts to explain crime and criminality.

Underpinning these theoretical developments and conflicts have been less obvious 'turf wars' between professional groups, for example that between psychologists and psychiatrists in the early days of the twentieth century. Awareness of early turf wars, that is battles for ownership of the dominant discourse within criminology, heightens awareness of current battles for control. Soothill shows us that general theories emerge and then fade, no matter how influential they have been in their time. He speculates, then, as to what future general theories might look like, and raises the possibility that the field of genetics might provide both the next influential theory and the next 'turf war' for ownership of the dominant discourse.

Situated in the present day, Chapter 2 argues that the media is now so all-pervasive in our lives that great care is required to disentangle what we know about crime and what we think we know. We have already stressed how crime is portrayed as exciting by the media. The influence of media in all our lives, not only in relation to crime, is widely discussed: so, for example, politicians are concerned about the extent to which we are influenced in our voting behaviour at elections both by television and newspapers.

As academics we need a language that can help us to understand the media and, in our case, its relation to crime. In Chapter 2, Moira Peelo argues for the importance of media representations in constructing public narratives about crime. Public narratives frame the social debate about crime in a mediated world. They provide a shared, recognised framework within which the contest for the control of the crime agenda takes place. Public narratives are, especially, a means of engaging with the emotionality surrounding public crime discourse.

Peelo argues that criminologists must learn to read the media at both a macro- and a micro-level to analyse the media products of a fragmented, pluralistic society in which there are multiple media choices. Such deconstruction that analyses visual and textual construction as well as its social context enables criminologists to recognise the continued presence of contest for control of the public crime agenda.

One currently recognised area of contention is that of the police and race relations. In Chapter 3, Simon Holdaway uses this example to explore the relationship between research and public agendas, questioning whether or not the sole role of criminology is to improve and change the world. Holdaway argues that it is not enough for criminologists to produce information (in this case 'outcomes' of who is stopped in the street). Rather, criminologists need to explore the processes and relationships that underlie such crime information. So, it is what one does with data that matters, rather than the existence of data alone.

Further, by taking a sociological approach, Holdaway explores 'institutional racism' in the light of detailed knowledge about the specific ways in which the institution (in this case, the police) is changing. His goal, in addition to a better understanding of police racism (hence, making the reality of improvement more possible) is to encourage criminologists to question radically the assumptions and theories underlying crime debate and phenomena.

The issue of police race relations is very much on the public agenda, but there are other fundamental relationships to confront. In Chapter 4 Chris Grover argues that any real attempt to tackle crime must start with recognising the relationships between inequality and crime. The comparative neglect of this relationship in recent times raises the question as to whether criminology is becoming too narrow in its interests. Grover is certainly making the plea that one needs to understand what is happening within a wider society in order to understand crime and crime-related phenomena.

Grover distinguishes between economic inequality and social inequality, and puts social justice firmly in the criminologists' frame. Criminologists, then, must take a sociological stance and understand, further, how social policy can, potentially, have negative impacts even when policy makers are attempting to address these issues.

Building on the radical criminology of the 1970s, Grover reminds us that the construction of social policy is not accidental, but reflects the economic needs of capital. Its needs are, therefore, reflected in measures intended to manage crime and offenders, and as criminologists we should, therefore, be able to analyse in detail the often competing assumptions embedded in policy. Not least, we should ensure that in a social period that emphasises personal responsibility and choice in offending behaviour we are not overlooking the real relationships between inequality and offending.

It is crucial at times to challenge the 'common-sense' knowledge of crime. What is crime to some is a rather different activity to others: hence, criminologists probe what must be recognised as the social construction of crime. Mike Presdee explores the meanings of transgression to offenders by using the example of 'arson' and, by examining this crime, questions what the breaking of socially constructed boundaries can mean.

Presdee usefully reminds us that, hitherto, criminologists have simply concentrated on the small number of offenders convicted of arson. He argues that there has been no real cultural analysis within criminology of the causes or genesis of arson. He maintains that a more cultural criminological approach can excavate the place and meaning of fire in a social and historical sense, bringing a greater depth and understanding to the question as to why at this time we are experiencing an increasing fascination with fire that results in both death and destruction.

His chapter explores meanings and cultural artefacts within a social context that places consumerism at the centre of identity. So it emphasises *how* we come to understand the human dimension. This approach is not a series of anecdotes for it places data within a framework for analysis.

Here, that framework is one of social construction and the separation of everyday life from the activities of the powerful – illustrating how the capacity to set boundaries invites transgression. So, in considering how we construct boundaries and how criminologists understand everyday life, Presdee opens up a new understanding of transgression.

Drugs represent a topic where populist politics have, for some years, been to the fore. Prohibition/legalisation, hard drugs/soft drugs are issues about which everyone seems to have a view. Most of the themes that underpin the development of this book emerge in Fiona Measham's chapter, which outlines the criminological issues surrounding drug use. This chapter has much to say concerning how societies construct illegality. So, for example, Measham argues that, while selective implementation of drug law may reflect popular opinion, laws cannot be abandoned just because many people commit those crimes. She compares, for instance, theft from shops and cannabis use. However, social change in the last 20 years has seen significant 'normalisation' of drug use, cannabis in particular moving from being deviant and subcultural to accommodation by the mainstream of society, which therefore demands a reconsideration of definitions of criminality and deviance.

Even where society is reasonably accommodating of drug use, this chapter illustrates how the law is implemented disproportionately. Young men and those from ethnic minorities are most likely to be convicted of drug-related offences. Like Grover, Measham questions the aims of social policy and legislation, asking whether drug-related laws and policies are intended to punish, to treat, to prevent drug use or to protect the rest of society from the repercussions of drug use. Drug policy is, she argues, an indicator of the compassion or humanity of a society and shapes how some of the most vulnerable in society are treated.

In Chapter 7, Brian Francis and Keith Soothill continue the consideration of social change. They highlight the important interlocking of understanding both data analysis and social change in their consideration of the 'delinquent generations' argument. It becomes clear that easy political answers to crime patterns, however tempting, cannot be effective unless terminology, methods of analysis and interpretation of data are understood. Clarity and care is needed in conceptualising, for example, differences between 'explanation' and 'prediction', and between 'age', 'cohort' and 'period' effect.

So, they present to us two competing (and highly politicised) explanations of changes in crime figures: that it is a generational matter caused by liberal 1960s parents ('cohort effect') and that there are yearly variations ('period effect'). Rather than arbitrating between these two viewpoints, they illustrate how neither can have meaning unless also disaggregated by age – hence age, period and cohort effects. In examining two case studies, Francis and Soothill show that criminologists need the skills to look behind models of change at the definitions assumed and the elements of social change acknowledged, or overlooked, to evaluate the real meaning of their findings.

Finally, David Lyon focuses on a topic that is peculiarly contemporary. Surveillance is an issue that has become increasingly controversial since the events of September 11, 2001 in New York. However, Lyon's chapter takes a wider view of what, to many, is a common-sense issue to do with monitoring and managing crime. He explores the issues surrounding governance, monitoring and policing in an information age. An example of how criminologists need to recognise changes in society, Lyon takes us beyond the human rights and privacy issues – important though these are – to a deeper understanding of the dualities of protection versus governance, of the need for societies to manage the new issues that arise from technological advances and solutions to earlier problems. We need, in effect, to be aware in detail of the political and ethical implications of crime measures, even where accepting of their uses.

From Lyon's perspective, surveillance for crime control is just one fraction of the monitoring and of the databases that hold information and which, ultimately, reconstruct us in manageable categories. Information societies are surveillance societies, in which the body disappears from integrative social relationships.

If the task of criminology is to explore and explain crime, then the chapters in this book are intended to enable students to develop a systematic, deeper style of questioning crime phenomena. While topics are wide-ranging, each chapter resonates with the themes we identified earlier. Our task has been to question 'what is crime?' and to remind readers of its socially constructed nature.

Further, it will be clear from this book that to explore crime and criminality effectively, students of criminology must come to terms with the dynamic, changing nature of society as well as of criminological theory. The historian, Herbert Butterfield, has argued that, 'the only absolute in history is change' (Haslam, 1999: 208). Interestingly, criminologists are sometimes reluctant to embrace social change – their methods and theories seem more ready to capture a static view of the world. This can be both misleading and possibly dangerous, for one must question what concepts of crime and criminality are consistent across all time and all societies.

By exploring a range of key criminological matters, *Questioning Crime and Criminology* is intended to help students go beyond an introductory level and to develop the tools by which, in the future, you can evaluate crime-related information at a deeper level. The aim is not to abolish all personal, instinctive opinion but rather to produce a million theorists, all of whom are able to disentangle complex crime information and come to their own conclusions – by a cogent and coherent route. Theorising is not the property of dead or dusty academics, but an activity that is open to all. Theorising starts with questioning – received wisdom, heavyweight philosophy, media images, 'common-sense' knowledge, academic research as well as populist political doctrines.

Theorising does require information, and to convince yourself with your own theory about crime phenomena needs, first, some grasp of what constitutes knowledge and what data implies. All academic studies require evidence to support a theoretical stance, and criminology is no different. Indeed, it is the systematic exploration of crime-related information that turns criminology into an exciting subject of study. Questioning crime and criminology carefully and in a detailed way is what, in the end, enables you to graduate with firm and informed foundations to your own theorising about crime, and *Questioning Crime and Criminology* is intended to help you do just that.

Chapter 1

Capturing criminology

Keith Soothill

Introduction

The aim of this chapter is simple. The task is to ensure that criminologists recognise that there have been various attempts in the past to 'capture' criminology. Such attempts are usually in the form of theories that are proffered to explain crime. The theories are so widely embracing that they are often referred to as 'general theories'. These 'general theories' attract much interest and attention with enthusiastic supporters, on the one hand, proclaiming the success of the endeavour while, on the other hand, opponents begin to cast doubt on the worth and the wisdom of a new approach to explanation. Certainly they often create conflict and controversy. While some theories do not produce much more than a ripple of interest, there are others that capture a place in the pantheon of criminology, so that the discipline of criminology is never quite the same again. The names of these theorists often crop up in textbooks of criminology, but their importance is perhaps not always clear.

The theories that purport to explain crime seem to have a limited life. In many respects they are the products of their time. Others come forward to challenge or modify current 'truths'. There will certainly be new ones in the future. Hence, studying the past has the dual purpose of enabling us to identify whether supposedly new theories are simply old theories dressed in some new clothes *and*, more crucially, providing us with knowledge of how the discipline has actually developed. Without such knowledge, questioning of contemporary criminology has little meaning.

The value of history

Two famous but misleading notions of history were stated within five years of each other. In 1916, the American car manufacturer, Henry Ford, stated, 'History is more or less bunk', going on to say that '… the only history that is worth a tinker's damn is the history we make today'.[1] In 1920, the British historian and biographer, Philip Guedalla, suggested, 'History repeats itself.'[2] We would be unwise to try to dismiss history – as Shakespeare says, 'There is a history in all … lives'[3] – while we would be equally unwise to expect easy answers from history. In fact, history has to be interpreted and there are various approaches to interpreting history. So, for example, a Marxist approach developed which challenged the positivist belief that the objective structure of reality was self-explanatory – that all that was necessary was to apply the methodology of science to it (Hobsbawm, 2005).

For social scientists, interpreting the world is more complex than that. Developing theories is one crucial aspect of trying to understand the social world. There are theorists who have tried to 'capture' criminology by proposing 'general theories' of crime. The question posed for this chapter is what do we learn from studying these 'general theories'? Are the ambitions of these theorists, indeed, too ambitious? Are there dangers? Should we lower our sights?

Foundations of criminology

We need to recognise that theorising is the motor of a discipline. Why is this so? Theorising helps us make sense of information, imposing some sort of order on what may appear to be a variety of information. It helps us to interpret, to analyse and to question. Without theory, the establishment of an academic discipline is perhaps questionable. Certainly Newton's observation of the falling apple – that contributed to his understanding of gravity – would not have made much of an impact on physics without the theorising that eventually accompanied the observation. Without history, one cannot understand what has gone before and the impact of the past on the present. Indeed, without history, one cannot appreciate the dangers of some earlier theorising in criminology. When one does understand, the cry of 'beware criminology' may have some potency.

There has been some important theorising in criminology. Some has been more influential than others, but the impact has been quite evident. What I call grandmasters (there have been no grandmistresses yet in criminology that have had the impact of these male theorists) have laid down key questions that can be still explored in different ways today. The ones considered here are those that theorise within the context of producing a 'general theory'. I raise the central concern of whether it is worth constructing a general theory of crime which leads to the question of whether we can in some way usefully integrate theories. With the example of Developmental and Life-Course Criminology (DLC), I later focus on this possibility. Meanwhile, of the grandmasters, the four I consider are Cesare Lombroso (1836–1909), Edwin Hardin Sutherland (1883–1950), Robert King Merton (1910–2003) and Travis Hirschi (b. 1935). Few could deny their importance and few would challenge the limitations of their theories, but nobody can do criminology seriously without coming to terms with their contributions and, indeed, the dangers of their contributions.

While very different in many ways, they all have one compelling appeal: at various times they have made criminology appear simple and straightforward. The other compelling feature of these theorists is that they – again in their different ways – tried to produce a general theory of crime.

First some prescriptions when one tries to address theory. Elsewhere (Soothill et al., 2002), we have stressed the importance of theorising and that, in criminology, theorising is about real people in the real world trying to make sense of the times in which they live. There we argued (pp. 98–9) that there are three basic questions worth considering when trying to get to grips with specific theoretical explanations:

1 What is the theory trying to explain, and therefore what aspects of the crime-criminal problem does it ignore?

2 How might we categorise this theory in relation to:
    – school of thought/periods of time;
    – key concepts and ideas;
    – main theorists?

3 When and where was the theory written? What was the potential influence of the social context at that time?

Lombroso

The social context of each of our grand theorists is crucial. Lombroso (born 1835 and died in 1909), often known as the 'father of criminology', was essentially responding to two demands – a popular belief that criminals are somehow different beings from the rest of us but also articulating that popular belief in what appeared to be the veneer of *scientific* explanation. Lombroso described how he was once standing with the skull of a notorious brigand in his hand and pondering over the problem of crime when suddenly the sun broke through the clouds and sunrays fell on the skull. Then, he said, it suddenly dawned on him that this skull and its anatomical structure provided the answer. For him there existed a distinct anthropological type, a born criminal, an individual likely or even bound to commit crime.

Lombroso's insights are easy targets nowadays for ridicule. However, what is important is that Lombroso was both implicitly and explicitly building on what has been termed the *positivist* viewpoint. Positivism is the contention that deviance (but usually, more specifically, criminality) can and should be studied by the methods of science. Certainly within criminology, 'the methods of science' have had a rather narrow interpretation. In fact, as it developed, the positivist position denied that offenders were responsible for their deeds, thus claiming that a punitive posture towards offenders is unjustified. This led on to the viewpoint that lawbreakers should be treated, not punished.

Pasquino (1991) suggests that the debate on what was then termed criminal anthropology shook the theoretical foundations of law and began to transform the perspectives of jurisprudence throughout the European continent, from Russia to Holland and Italy. He suggests that the defining moment for the start of this debate began in 1885 when Enrico Ferri delivered a university lecture on 'The positivist school of criminology'. Ferri was an academic and a jurist, a pupil of Lombroso and the most active and best-known member of the Italian legal school. It is said that during his lecture there emerged a new figure – *homo criminalis* – which was outside the sphere of classical penal thought. In classical theory, penal justice is constructed around a triangle formed by law, crime and punishment. However, what is of interest about this triangle of law, crime and punishment is the absence of the figure of the criminal. What occupies its place is the postulate of a 'free will' that establishes the subjective basis of the power to punish. As free will is common to all (i.e. to every juridical subject), it is hence not the object of a special form of knowledge. Within that classical tradition that is now seen as pre-positivist thinking, anyone can commit a crime, for it exists as a potentiality in each of us. Committing crime is, therefore, regarded as a *rational* process – we can decide to do so or not. In fact, Pasquino stresses how from the 1870s and 1880s, the essential elements of the old penal rationality began to be dramatically overturned, as there was growing concern about the impotence of punishments and the rising number of crimes. The new approach of positivism was the outcome.

The problem came to be posed in terms of the origin or aetiology of crime. As Pasquino stresses, at the heart of the new theory was Darwinism whereby it was posited that a social organism could exhibit different stages of the evolution of the species. By this account, criminals can be identified as archaic residues who are unable to keep up with the proper pace of evolution and are left behind by it. Lombroso was essentially arguing that heredity was the principal cause of criminal tendencies. However, his main legacy is his focus on the criminal rather than the crime. In his famous lecture in Naples, Ferri – echoing his teacher – said that the criminal is naturally a savage, and socially an abnormal. In other words, Ferri was arguing that the criminal simply does not think like a normal and honest person. Hence, a different explanation is required.

So what was to be done, given the supposed impotence of punishments and the rising number of crimes? For Ferri, the answer lay in the elimination of the very sources of crime, namely the criminal. The new theory began to be concerned far less with dissuading the citizen from law breaking than with rendering the criminal incapable of harm. The question was what to do with these evil and dangerous persons?

One line of development reflected Ferri's proposal to send hardened criminals to reclaim the marshes of Latium, where they would perish of malaria, thereby ridding society of them for good. As Pasquino notes, this suggestion was actually put into effect during the fascist era in Italy. In fact, Ferri's own move from joining the Socialist Party as a young progressive in the 1880s to becoming a convert to the fascist regime in Italy is not without interest.

There is, then, one other important aspect of the heritage of Lombroso that needs to be recognised. Both implicitly and explicitly Lombroso is claiming the sovereignty of medical discourse, with a biological slant, over traditional legal discourse in enabling us to understand crime and criminals. This shift of discourse provides the context for many of the historical fights within criminology, for this is the source of the simple, but wrong, assertion that 'scientific research' can be equated with the medical model. Such fights, dressed up in various forms of battledress, can more colloquially be seen as 'turf battles'.

Understanding 'turf battles' – that is, who owns the dominant discourse within criminology – is an interesting way of considering the contributions of the three grandmasters (Sutherland, Merton and Hirschi) who, with their general theories, tried to 'capture' criminology. Essentially 'turf battles' are about professional competition and there are some important battles before the 1930s when Sutherland and Merton came more prominently onto the scene.

Turf battles

Nicole Rafter (1997) identifies the important historical point that theories of crime causation changed rapidly in the early twentieth century. Rafter has persuasively located this evolution of criminology in the context of the history of the professions. The changes occurred against a backdrop of competition between psychologists and psychiatrists for the authority to identify and classify offenders. Rafter's work identifies the battle between these two professions who are both working within the medical model, but this type of analysis can embrace other professions and disciplines.

Psychology was an immature but ambitious profession when Henry H. Goddard, one of the first clinical psychologists, decided to invade the jurisdiction of the criminal anthropologist which was still championing the notion of an atavistic, physically stigmatised born criminal (Goddard, 1914). Using Binet's new intelligence tests, Goddard popularised the feeble-mindedness explanation of criminal behaviour. In fact, Goddard's work on *The Kallikak Family* (originally published in 1912) had attempted to show that mental deficiency was inherited according to Mendelian law.[4] In establishing links with crime, pauperism and prostitution, Goddard maintained that it was specifically feeble-mindedness which was transmitted. The evidence was limited but superficially impressive. Goddard had traced two lines of descent from Martin Kallikak – one normal, the other feeble-minded.

Martin Kallikak, a soldier in the American Revolutionary War, had a child by 'an unmarried feeble-minded girl', and after the War married a 'Quaker girl from an honest and intelligent family'. Some 496 descendants of the Quaker girl were traced, Goddard asserted, among whom there were no criminals, and all except one had been mentally normal. However, of the 486 descendants of the feeble-minded girl that were traced, Goddard claimed that '36 have been illegitimate, 33 sexually immoral persons, mostly prostitutes; 24 alcoholics, 3 epileptics; 82 died in infancy, 3 criminals and 8 kept houses of ill-fame'. The detail is not to encourage us to applaud the industry of Goddard, but to recognise a line of reasoning and an empirical approach that may become fashionable again in the twenty-first century with the increasingly emerging discipline of genetics. In short, the emperor may soon have a new set of clothes.

Psychiatry, a much older profession than psychology, had become stagnant in the late nineteenth century, a specialty practised mainly inside lunatic asylums by administrators more interested in controlling patients than treating them. However, a new generation of reform psychiatrists was emerging, hoping to wrest the specialty away from the asylum superintendents, making it much more clinically useful and moving the practice of psychiatry into the community. Psychopathy – a concept derived from German psychiatry – provided the reformers with a vehicle for promoting these goals and making psychiatry relevant to criminal justice. In Rafter's words, 'psychopathy became the Trojan horse in which psychiatrists entered the criminological territory of psychologists' (pp. 239–40).

Rafter explains how, in the United States, the most influential and extensive early twentieth century discussions of psychopathy appeared in works by the psychiatrists Bernard Glueck (1884–1972) – who was also the brother and brother-in-law to the famous criminologists, Sheldon and Eleanor Glueck – William Healy (who studied juveniles – both male and female) and Edith R. Spaulding (who focused on adult female psychopaths). These were all engaged in a new attempt to explain how criminals differed from law-abiding citizens. The late nineteenth century criminal anthropologists had tried but failed to establish the nature of the criminal's abnormality as, indeed, at the beginning of the twentieth century had the new mental-testing psychologists. Around 1915, reform psychiatrists in search of a broader clientele away from the old lunatic asylums began explaining *criminal* abnormality in terms of psychopathy. The crucial 'differentness' of criminals was conceptualised – whether by psychiatrists or psychologists – as being *within* the individual.

The implications of these kinds of approaches, which locate criminality in genetic, constitutional or inherited psychological characteristics and thus solely *within* individuals, are important. They identify social problems as lying beyond social or economic factors, and hence develop a quasi-medical programme in trying to create a solution to the crime problem. In suggesting that social factors are largely immaterial, explanations that emerge from the biological and heredity realm are essentially conservative, for their solutions to crime and social problems do not impinge on or challenge existing patterns of the distribution of wealth. For such explanations of challenge one needs to turn to other disciplines, most notably sociology.

Sutherland

The battle now becomes one of calling upon the social as opposed to genetic or heredity explanations. In the late 1930s two new 'grandmasters' came to the fore. They developed two related but rather distinct contributions. Their essential challenge was to the notion of abnormality and, in their different ways, considered the criminal to be behaving 'normally'. I will first consider Edwin Sutherland whom Hermann Mannheim (1965) claimed would be one of the most deserving candidates for a Nobel Prize if there were one for criminology. Mannheim's putative crowning with a Nobel Prize was based on Sutherland's work in identifying and establishing the problem of white-collar crime. This was, in fact, a massive challenge to conventional wisdom, for Sutherland was arguing that crime was not a peculiarly lower-class phenomenon but a feature of all classes. The importance of Sutherland's contribution in reframing the *definition* of crime has perhaps not always been fully recognised or, indeed, acted upon.

However, beyond introducing the crucial concept of white-collar crime, Sutherland had much more on his agenda. He had been heavily influenced by a critique of criminology written in 1933 by Jerome Michael and Mortimer J. Adler that argued that criminology had failed to produce sound scientific evidence and had no coherent theories. Further, Sutherland had recognised that the 1930s were characterised by the increasing dominance of psychological explanations of criminal activity. A developing interest in psychoanalysis had certainly been given a massive boost in Britain by the arrival of Sigmund Freud as a Jewish refugee from the atrocities of the Nazis in Europe prior to the Second World War. As the works of Freud and his disciples were published and became available in English, their views became more influential. One can see the passion with which Sutherland was challenging the psychoanalytic approach:

> Business leaders are capable, emotionally balanced, and in no sense pathological. We have no reason to think that General Motors has an inferiority complex or that the Aluminium Company of America has a frustration–aggression complex or that U.S. Steel has an Oedipus complex, or that the Armour Company has a death wish or that Du Ponts desire to return to the womb. The assumption that an offender must have some such pathological distortion of the intellect or the emotions seems to me absurd, and if it is absurd regarding the crimes of businessmen, it is equally absurd regarding the crimes of persons in the lower economic class. (Mannheim, 1965, but originally from *The Sutherland Papers*, p. 96 [from an unpublished paper of 1948 on 'Crime of Corporations']).

We have little or no evidence one way or the other whether business leaders are, indeed, 'emotionally balanced'. However, the point remains that the main burden for explaining white-collar crime seems unlikely to fall upon psychological approaches, partly because the problems are widespread and so cannot be explained as aberrations.

As a direct challenge to medical explanations and seeing crime as pathological, Sutherland made a bold attempt to produce a general theory of crime. First advanced in 1924 (Downes and Rock, 1998), Sutherland proposed his theory of differential association by which he argued that deviance is a way of life passed from generation to generation. Differential association is essentially a theory based on the social environment and its surrounding individuals and the values those individuals gain from significant others in their social environment. Drawn from the theories and approaches of the early work of the Chicago School, Sutherland's own work included the ecological and transmission theory, symbolic inter-actionism and culture conflict. However, in the quest to understand crime causation, it can be regarded as a social learning approach – that is, criminal behaviour is learned behaviour and is learned via social interaction. By emphasising the 'social' rather than simply focusing on individual development, he developed a social learning theory that attempted to explain not only individual criminal behaviour but also that of social groups.

Importantly, Hollin (2002: 150) notes[5] how, despite the fact that American psychology was shifting towards behaviourism, 'in which the clear focus would be the power of the environment in shaping behaviour', Sutherland's theory curiously failed to make an impact on psychologists interested in explanations of crime. Instead, among psychologists, the relationship between physique and crime became both popular and central to their interests. As Hollin insightfully records, 'at a key point psychology failed to connect with criminology and the opportunity for a genuine academic alliance slipped away' (Hollin, 2002: 150).

Merton

The contribution of our third 'grandmaster', Robert K. Merton, can easily be understood within the Rafter approach of locating the evolution of criminology in the context of the history of the professions. Merton provides an unashamedly sociological approach to an understanding of deviance in general and crime in particular. In charting the move in criminology towards considering social process and social structure, Merton is a pivotal figure.

In contrast to Sutherland, Robert Merton is known much more widely than for his writings in the area of crime and deviance. His wide-ranging contributions also shaped such fields of study as bureaucracy, communications and propaganda, social psychology, social stratification and the relationship between science, technology and society. His death in 2003 aged 92 produced a remarkable set of obituaries in national newspapers, typically declaring that he 'was, perhaps, the last of an extraordinary generation of American sociologists whose work shaped the basic definition of the discipline in the mid-20th century' (Calhoun, 2003).

As Calhoun notes, Merton's life portrays a very American trajectory (appropriate to his date of birth in 1910). His parents were Jewish immigrants from eastern Europe. Named Meyer Schkolnick at birth, he changed his name when he won a scholarship to the local Temple University. His publications were extraordinarily influential, displaying 'the virtues of clarity and sheer intellectual creativity' (Calhoun, 2003).

As a student, the writings of the French sociologist, Emile Durkheim, had a great impact on Merton. Durkheim believed that individuals possessed an unlimited appetite of aspirations and it was up to society to regulate this appetite. If appropriate regulation failed or was weakened, Durkheim had argued that a state of anomie would occur, whereby the limitless appetites of individuals would be unleashed and a variety of deviant behaviours was likely to result. After reading Durkheim's work, 'Merton assigned himself the task of discovering what produces anomie' (Hunt, 1961: 58).

Merton's eventual challenge was profound, for implicitly he was questioning the American dream of prosperity for many, perhaps most, of its citizens. While the United States with its huge influx of immigrants in the first decades of the twentieth century was seen as the land of opportunity, the American dream was not equally attainable for everyone. When Merton began writing his seminal article, 'Social Structure and Anomie' (1938), the Great Depression was still in everyone's memory.

In developing Durkheim's concept of anomie, Merton stated there are two elements of social and cultural structure, which essentially relate to ends and means. The ends are the culturally assigned goals and aspirations (Merton, 1938: 672), which individuals expect out of life, such as material success. The means are the ways that are defined by the social structure as appropriate for people to get what they want out of life. People are expected to seek an education and then by hard work to achieve their goals. The crucial point is that the culturally desired goals of material success should be achievable by legitimate means for all social classes. However, if goals are not equally achievable through legitimate means, illegitimate means might then be used to achieve the same goals. The problems are said to occur when there is too much disparity between goals and means. In other words, if material success is emphasised and there are not the opportunities to achieve this goal legally, then crime provides another route for this success to be achieved. Hence crime, for Merton, largely comes about through failings in the social structure rather than through individual failings.

Merton's 1938 article and its subsequent revisions became the most cited work in criminology and had an enormous impact. Pfohl (1994) points to how Merton's work was influential in framing some of the social programmes in the United States in the 1960s, such as affirmative action and equal opportunity. However, the programme that was more specifically ascribed to Merton's influence was 'Mobilization for Youth' that emerged during the Kennedy administration. Based on the Mertonian principle of opportunity, the aim of the programme was to attack socially structured obstacles for youths in a lower-class Manhattan neighbourhood.

Pfohl (1994: 278) suggests that the Mobilization for Youth programme may have been too radical for its time. While there was no marked improvement in delinquency, the lower classes began to learn to bond together and to challenge what they did not agree with. This was a development that neither the government nor the criminological theory of the time could readily cope with. Nevertheless, Merton's work produced challenges that influenced criminology greatly.

In an emerging challenge to the then dominant approach of functional analysis represented by Robert Merton and his teacher, Talcott Parsons, that resonated throughout sociology in the 1950s, Howard Becker would perhaps be seen by most as the inspirational figure who was pivotal to a shift of direction in the 1960s in the field of crime and deviance. However, despite his renewal of the symbolic interactionist perspective of G. H. Mead and what came to be known as 'labelling theory' (a term that Becker himself despised – see Becker, 1973), Becker and his colleagues were challenging 'grand theories' rather than creating one. Their insights into social processes and social reactions to crime charted the way for a more anthropological perspective on crime that readily embraced qualitative methods as part of the canon of scientific techniques.

Hirschi

More low-key in its time but potentially more explosive was the theme being developed by Travis Hirschi, whose work in his book *Causes of Delinquency* (1969) seemed at first glance to be just reporting an empirical study. However, the work presages much more than was originally recognised by most. While correctly identified as laying the foundation for Hirschi's control theory, it had an even more fundamental mission. It challenged the way that we should think about crime and criminology and in this respect he emerges as our fourth 'grandmaster'. Hirschi was indeed questioning whether criminology was posing the right question. He turned the usual question on its head. He suggested that, instead of asking why someone committed a crime – which needed a special motivational account of crime and delinquency – we should ask why someone would not commit crime. In other words, unless there were reasons not to, we would all commit crime and so there was no need to consider a special motivational account for crime.

This is essentially a return to the classical approach which Lombroso and his disciples had so effectively, but misleadingly, challenged. Hirschi is known as a control theorist within this tradition and has presented two major versions of control theory in his academic career. The first version developed in 1969 proposed that weak social bonds may set an individual free to weigh up the benefits of crime. The second version principally developed in 1990 with Michael Gottfredson in *A General Theory of Crime* focuses more on self-control rather than social control as the root of criminality. The emphasis on self-control has in turn produced a focus on parental upbringing as the main source of socialisation that instils self-control in a child.

Gottfredson and Hirschi's work promotes a more genuinely inter-disciplinary approach to crime. So the central thesis of their interdisciplinary approach is that theories of crime that are, say, solely sociological ignore individual traits that account for a significant, if not the major, proportion of variation in individual criminal activities. For Gottfredson and Hirschi, the causally important *individual* trait is self-control. However, the theory proposed by Gottfredson and Hirschi in fact combines elements of opportunity and control theories (1990: 23). From opportunity theory, the proposition is taken that environmental conditions influence criminal opportunities. So, for example, the availability of suitably attractive and unguarded targets influences whether particular crimes are likely to occur. But from control theory, the proposition is borrowed that people differ in their *propensity* to take advantage of criminal opportunities. According to the theory, persons with low self-control are more likely to steal what is just lying around than those with high self-control. In this view, then, the two major causal factors that explain crime are self-control and opportunity.

According to this theory, the only motive involved in crime is something akin to greed, that is the desire to pursue one's short-term pleasure, gratification or gain. And where does this motive come from? The motive derives from an *internal* characteristic of the individual – low self-control (in other words, there are no *external* pressures which variations of strain theories may suggest help to constrain people to do certain things).

The later theory has attracted remarkable interest and popularity. This is partly political and partly theoretical. The political is easy to under-stand. It emerged in the early 1990s when conservative values, particularly in the support of the nuclear family, were paramount. To espouse effective state policies that would support the family and the quality of family child-rearing practices was certainly less challenging than to espouse theories that might challenge the social structure. Also, in a climate when retributive punishments were in favour, to hear that public policies that were designed to deter or rehabilitate offenders would continue to fail supported a popular polemic among conservative politicians.

The theory also attracts ready interest because it is simple to understand and purports to be an all-embracing theory about crime. However, this is a pernicious combination that spells trouble. The problem with Gottfredson and Hirschi's general theory of crime – which is shared with most other general theories of crime – is that there is enough support from empirical work to encourage its supporters, but not enough to convince concerned opposition.

Certainly the theory's major conclusion that low self-control is related to criminal involvement can hardly be disputed, but an association of this kind is very different from an assertion of a general causative link for *all* offenders. In claiming quite definitively that white-collar crime can be included in their general theory, however, evidence in this area undermines their general theory. As Benson and Moore (1992) argue, many individuals in white-collar crime have demonstrated they can cope with delayed gratification – the opposite of low self-control – by achieving an advanced education.

The conservative undertones of the approach – with the espousal of the traditional roles of men and women, with the man working during the day and the woman staying at home – have nostalgic appeal to many but are totally unrealistic in contemporary society. Furthermore, to posit self-control as the general concept around which all of the known facts about crime can be organised seems both limited and limiting. However, it is fair to add that their perspective is not meant to predict any single act of crime or deviance, for, after all, they maintain that crime is impulsive and opportunistic. They are simply saying that lack of control and the family's role in its failed development provide the circumstances and conditions that are favourable for delinquency. Their reluctance to engage with other and possibly competing explanations about crime – in the belief that they have said the last word – suggests that the influence of their theory will increasingly wane.

The four grandmasters identified are all important figures in the history of criminology. In their different ways they have attempted to produce a 'grand theory' that purports to be an explanation of all crime. It is now perhaps easy to see each theorist as a product of his time, challenging the current orthodoxies. Both their insights and their challenges remain influential, but the overall acceptance of any of their general theories is more questionable. Indeed, is the postulation of a general theory the way forward for criminology or should we be taking another route? Currently the major competing approach comes from those who claim they want more integration among theories. In this respect it is appropriate to focus upon those who espouse developmental and life-course criminology.

The possibility of integrating theoretical approaches

Developmental and life-course criminology is perhaps beginning to make an impact, because it promises to fill a massive gap. Just as political regimes fall and one asks what to put in their place, so some recent enthusiasms within criminology seem to have run out of steam. The enthusiasm for Marxist criminology in the early 1970s had many important spin-offs, but soon seemed itself to spin off into a hinterland. The situational criminology, espoused by the Home Office in the early 1980s, had similarly seemed to run its course. The limitations of the 'risk factor prevention paradigm' within criminology, which developed in the early 1990s as a response to wider concerns about risk, were being recognised. It certainly had limited use as an explanation of crime.

A more recent interest has been to move away from claims of producing a general theory of crime and to argue that various theoretical approaches can be usefully integrated. The claim of a desire for more integration may, of course, mask other intentions, whether conscious or not. It may be a way of playing out turf battles in another form. In other words, integration may involve the coming together of what may be seen as equal partners or, more perniciously, the domination of one approach over another – more crudely, is it assimilation or conquest? Certainly one needs to consider who is offering to integrate! In most current examples one can perhaps recognise that some psychologists are in effect challenging for the heart and soul of criminology, while offering olive branches to some other disciplines with an interest in criminology. While there are various contenders who purport to be leading criminology to a more enlightened position, David Farrington, Professor of Psychological Criminology at Cambridge University, has recently made an important statement on key theoretical and empirical issues relating to the integration of theoretical approaches (Farrington, 2003).

Farrington, the only person to achieve the presidency of both the American Society of Criminology and the British Society of Criminology, has a curious position in British criminology. His antipathy towards speaking to the media has meant that he is not well known to an audience beyond criminology and those engaged in crime policy. Nevertheless, he is the most cited criminology author working in Britain who has built up his reputation through careful stewardship of the Cambridge Development Study since the retirement of Donald West, the founder of the study. However, his work has also been extensive in collaborating with other studies, particularly in the United States. He carried the banner of empirical work in Britain for many years but, perhaps because the Cambridge study has been heavily supported by the Home Office, he has been categorised by many as an atheoretical administrative criminologist. However, the support of the Home Office certainly helped his work to be influential in the development of crime policies in the 1990s, particularly in relation to some of the initiatives of New Labour, and Farrington's work would help to challenge any view that criminology has been sidelined in the *official* arena. Nevertheless, his reluctance to court or even respond to the media has not helped criminology in the *public* arena. Furthermore, his work is not quoted extensively in introductory criminology courses and his material to date is much more likely to be the focus of more specialised second- or third-year options.

The reason for this is straightforward. Criminology teaching has been dominated by those espousing a more sociological background where explanations are more at the societal level. In contrast, Farrington at Cambridge and many influential criminologists working in the Home Office in the 1980s and 1990s have a background in psychology. While recognising the importance of the social context, their interests have focused more on explaining crime at the individual level.

Currently, Farrington seems anxious to claim a theoretical position. Indeed, on receiving the prestigious Sutherland Award, he states 'in recognition of Edwin H. Sutherland's great theoretical contribution, I decided to concentrate on theory [in my lecture]' (Farrington, 2003). The 2002 Sutherland Award Address provides a useful exemplar in attempting to integrate approaches. His focus is on what he calls 'Developmental and life-course criminology (DLC)', stressing that DLC is 'especially concerned with documenting and explaining within-individual changes in offending throughout life' (p. 221). In fact, he sees the approach as specifically 'concerned with three main issues: the development of offending and antisocial behaviour, risk factors at different ages, and the effects of life events on the course of development'.

Farrington argues that DLC incorporates 'three other paradigms with slightly different emphases that became prominent in the 1990s'. Here he includes the risk factor prevention paradigm, developmental criminology and life-course criminology. What he is attempting that is different is to identify the key elements that he maintains should be included in any DLC theory.[6]

Farrington sets out clearly the key empirical questions that need to be addressed by any DLC theory (see Box 1.1). Farrington's baker's dozen of questions reveals the empirical substance of his concerns and, by extension, that of DLC theories. The issue of interest here is with the questions posed rather than the possible answers, for we need to ask whether the questions chart the boundaries of criminology. Indeed, if these questions are answered, would it then be a general theory of crime?

In his Sutherland Award address Farrington launches the latest development of his DLC theory that he calls the 'Integrated Cognitive Antisocial Potential' (ICAP) theory. Figure 1.1 shows the key elements of the ICAP theory in a simplified form. Its key construct is antisocial potential (AP), and it assumes that 'the translation from anti-social potential to antisocial behavior depends on cognitive (thinking and decision-making) processes that take account of opportunities and victims' (Farrington, 2003: 231). Impressively, it claims to integrate 'ideas

---

Box 1.1

Key DLC issues to be addressed

1. Why do people start offending?
2. How are onset sequences explained?
3. Why is there continuity in offending from adolescence to adulthood?
4. Why do people stop offending?
5. Why does prevalence peak in the teenage years?
6. Why does an early onset predict a long criminal career?
7. Why is there versatility in offending and antisocial behavior?
8. Why does co-offending decrease from adolescence to adulthood?
9. Why are there between-individual differences in offending?
10. What are the key risk factors for onset and desistance, and how can they be explained?
11. Why are there within-individual differences in offending:
    (a) long term (over life)?
    (b) short term (over time and place)?
12. What are the main motives and reasons for offending?
13. What are the effects of life events on offending?

Source: Farrington (2003: 229–30).

---

from many other theories, including strain, control, learning, labelling, and rational choice approaches' (ibid.).

It is, in fact, a brave and thoughtful attempt to codify and provide a framework for what is known within life-course criminology. However, the approach raises at least three concerns.

Firstly, it is ironic that Farrington uses the occasion of the Sutherland Award – named in honour of the man who challenged the criminological focus on lower-class offending – to launch a new version of his DLC version which is explicitly designed to explain offending by *lower-class males*. Certainly it will help to prolong the belief that the main focus of criminology should be on the offending of lower-class males.

Secondly, by being more specific, it is certainly not a general theory in the way that the grandmasters attempted. However, like Sutherland, its focus goes beyond crime as a legal category and widens its embrace to cover antisocial behaviour in its explanation of within-individual changes in behaviour throughout life. Nevertheless, while in theory this could

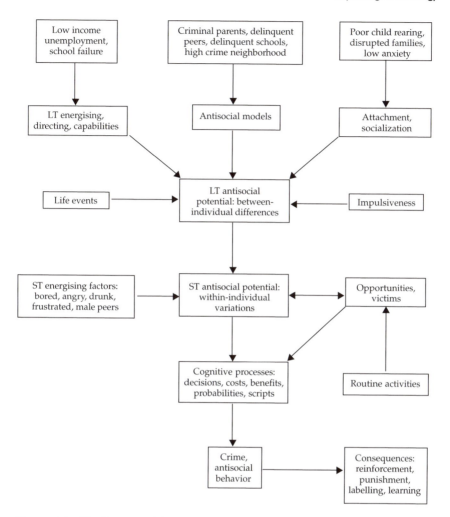

Figure 1.1 The Integrated Cognitive Antisocial Potential (ICAP) theory.
Source: Farrington (2003: 232).

include the anti-social behaviour of all classes, there is little doubt that again the main force of the approach is directed towards the control of the lower orders.

However, the third concern is the most important. We must not be trapped into thinking that criminology should be bounded by the questions posed by Farrington and outlined in Box 1.1. The focus there is essentially on known criminals and how we understand their trajectories through life. However, there is more to criminology than that. Stanley Cohen memorably stated that 'The stuff of criminology consists of only three questions: Why are laws made? Why are they broken? What do we do or what should we do about this?' (Cohen, 1988: 9). This usefully reminds us that general theories have, in fact, been rather limited. The challenge is as much about understanding the social construction of crime as it is about simply embracing a narrow focus on the criminal.

In fact, a narrow focus on the criminal represents some dangerous waters that criminology seems about to enter. There is much around that is beginning to suggest that our first grandmaster, Cesare Lombroso, will begin to be revered again rather than to be ridiculed. Lombroso's focus on the criminal with a neglect of the social context of crime has increasingly a contemporary resonance.

A general theory emerges in the context of its time and I suspect that the next generation of general theories is likely to emerge from the so-called genetics revolution that is currently taking place. There are vast amounts of money being spent on genetics research and new turf battles about the supremacy of particular explanations. Importantly, genetics seems a seductively simple way to explain human behaviour in general and criminal behaviour in particular. Criminologists will need to remember all the lessons they have learned about the social construction of crime, so that they can resist the worst excesses of a general theory of crime based on genetics.

While in the final analysis general theories always fail, they can still have great impact in the interim, both negative and positive. The positive impact is usually that general theories help to remind us of factors that have been neglected. Certainly the impact of heredity may have been underestimated in many accounts of the development of human be-haviour, but its importance in the analysis of crime and criminal behaviour can easily be exaggerated. Indeed, the message from this brief overview of general theories of crime is that the danger for criminology begins to be serious when the search for a general causal theory is thought to be successful and completed. It is then that the questioning really needs to be intense.

Notes

1 Henry Ford in an interview with Charles N. Wheeler, *Chicago Tribune*, 25 May 1916 (taken from Partington, 1992: 289).
2 Philip Guedalla (1920) 'Some historians', in *Supers and Supermen* (taken from Partington, 1992: 319).
3 William Shakespeare (1597) *Henry I, Part 2*, Act III, scene 1, line 80.
4 Gregor Mendel (1822–84) was an Austrian monk – acclaimed as the founder of genetics – who studied the peas that he grew in the monastery garden. He turned the study of the way in which traits are inherited into a science. From

his findings – that remained unrecognised until the early twentieth century – he formulated his law of segregation and law of independent assortment of characters, which are now recognised as two of the fundamental laws of heredity (Nicholls, 1996).

5 In this important student textbook, Sutherland is incorrectly noted as being born in 1853 rather than in 1883. He was, in fact, at the height of his powers when he died in 1950 with his famous book, *White Collar Crime*, having been published in the previous year.

6 Farrington points to DLC theories by Catalano and Hawkins (1996), Sampson and Laub (1993), Moffitt (1993), LeBlanc (1997) and Thornberry and Krohn (2001) as well as citing Loeber's (1996) developmental pathways theory, Wikström's (1995) self-control/temptation/friction theory, Lahey and Waldman's (2003) developmental propensity model and the coercion/early onset model of Patterson (Weisner et al., 2003) as fellow-travellers.

Chapter 2

Crime and the media: public narratives and private consumption

Moira Peelo

Introduction

Crime is one of the most popular consumer products of our times. Packaged for newspapers, TV and film drama, crime is everywhere both as news items and as entertainment; and news, in spite of its often solemn wrapping, provides entertainment too. We know about crime and hear about crime everyday through the all-pervasive presence of media in our lives. This ever-present public knowledge produces important challenges to criminologists: to analyse carefully how we know about crime, and to evaluate exactly what it is that we know.

The importance of media representations of crime has long been recognised: Reiner (2002) has outlined the large volume of criminological writing on the subject. Reiner usefully separates his overview into the content, consequences and causes of media representations of crime, as a way of guiding the reader through the maze, because each 'has been the basis for a voluminous literature attempting to analyse the content, effects, and sources of media crime' (p. 377). But rather than acknowledge the embedded nature of media within society, criminologists traditionally attempt to separate out individual media and their specific impacts. So, for example, Reiner outlines the numerous studies trying to establish the impact of media specifically on crime behaviour (as a cause of offending) and on fear of crime (often viewed as part of alarmist political strategies).

Perhaps, however, it is sociologists who show us the way forward in framing this discussion; for example, Abercrombie et al. (2000) argue that media are so embedded in ordinary life that we hardly notice the extent of what has been both a technological and an information revolution (pp. 367–8). This embeddedness of media makes the study of individual media and their direct impact on behaviour and feelings about crime too limited for real meaning in criminology. So how can criminologists usefully enter this massively changing media world and what analysis provides the most appropriate approach? In this chapter I will argue that it is public narratives that criminologists must explore to gain understanding of how societies discuss and make sense of crime issues and images, and by which to recognise the socially constructed nature of our understanding of crime.

Background

The generality that must matter to criminologists, then, is the nature of the crime debate in a mediated society, that is the nature of public narratives in a social world for which the key crime issues and their conflicts are framed substantially through the processes of mediation. As Altheide and Snow (1979) have argued, '… social reality is constituted, recognized, and celebrated with media' (p. 12). In this wider discussion it is not only the nature of individual media that matters, we also need to recognise *the centrality of mediation in the construction of knowledge about crime*. Hence, it is possible, then, for Altheide and Snow to claim that '… in contemporary society the logic of media provides the form for shared "normalized" social life' (p. 12). This means, for us as members of society, that shared life is mediated through numerous channels (media, in this sense, include such as telephones and computers in addition to the more obvious media of television, radio, film and newspaper). As well as making us subject to a rich range of information, images and ideas unknown in humanity's earlier history, media provide us with a shared public life that is recognised as standard. In fact, given the all-encompassing nature of mediated images – in this instance those of crime – it makes sense that we use these images as the currency through which we exchange and argue our viewpoints. This framing of public narratives is not as straightforward as framing *individual* viewpoints; rather it is Altheide and Snow's social reality – 'constituted, recognized, and celebrated' crime phenomena. Mediated images become the language of Altheide and Snow's 'shared "normalized" social life'.

All this is happening within the context of considerable changes to both society and mass media production in the last thirty years. These must be acknowledged if we are to make sense of the media–crime dimension. So, for example, globalisation, cross-ownership of media outlets and changes in the competitiveness of the media marketplace have helped to escalate the blurring of edges between the outputs of various media, both fictional and factually based, in their treatment of crime. Reiner has acknowledged that the 'current stage of development reflects the impact of the more general features of 'postmodernity' on the relationship between media, crime and criminal justice' (p. 407). One of the features he identifies is the blurring of boundaries between fictional and factual accounts; another is the contest between various groups – including criminal justice agencies – for the media's news agenda. Reiner points out how the terrorist attacks on New York of September 11, 2001, illustrate how crime can be constructed with the media in mind, and hence it is not just the traditional justice agencies that now construct their activities in the light of media attention. Crime is an important commodity in the engagement of public interest (as it has been for many centuries), an end which has been increasingly sought by both politicians and media producers. There has been, at the same time, an escalation of the interweaving of fictionalised crime events, fiction based on crime-related phenomena, politicisation of crime and competition for the news reporting agenda – and all in the name of personal consumption.

So, for example, the relatively unknown subject of women in prison has been dealt with in a number of ways. The seamless move between fiction and real life is played out on television: *Prisoner: Cell Block H* gave way to *Bad Girls*, the first a TV soap-cum-drama series from Australia, the second a drama series-cum-soap set in a British prison. *Bad Girls* played off *Footballers' Wives*, as glamorous characters, created to inhabit the wealthy world of a TV drama series focusing on football, moved from one to the other via a fictional case of murder. This gave way in 2004 to another TV documentary series set in a women's prison – Bullwood Hall – and the series was called *The Real Bad Girls*. To place this 'reality' TV, one has to understand the fictional account – the two are irretrievably bound together via their titles in a form of intratextuality. But there is no glamour in Bullwood Hall.

Meanwhile, in the same year, a Sunday newspaper, the *Observer*, was running a campaign about the plight of women prisoners and the state of their prisons. In this version of women's prisons there is a history of distress, mental illness, suicide, self-harm, drugs and family disintegration. So bad are their prisons that Martin Narey, then Home Office head of correctional services, was described as aiming to move women out of many existing prisons because of the dire conditions (*Observer*, 25 July 2004, p. 10). Hence, different media use their technologies and forms to different ends in the use of crime-related stories. Yet, even in the *Observer*'s campaigning story about the unhappy lives of *ordinary* women in prison, the accompanying photographs include those of Myra Hindley and Rose West, two exceptionally notorious prisoners – hence sensationally reminding readers of two sets of killings.

Within a postmodernist framework of analysis one might expect the fragmentation of society, plus the plethora of media choices, to allow varied audiences to interact differently according to the medium, the story and the crime. Yet, alongside this variety found in a pluralistic world, there are common threads and shared knowledge, as illustrated by easy recognition of exceptional cases such as the West and Moors murders (implied in the use of Rose West and Myra Hindley's photographs). These common threads contribute to the shape of public narratives, within which contest for control of the public debate about crime takes place.

Public narratives

Public narratives mark the acknowledged parameters of a society's crime debate at a given moment in time (including, paradoxically, what is not discussed). They form the currently recognised framework for contest in the public arena, the ring within which the fight for the crime agenda takes place. Shared acceptance of the language of public narratives should not be mistaken for social homogeneity or agreement about crime. Public narratives are, to borrow Altheide and Snow's thinking, the recognisable text of understood values, made up of a shared language about crime in a highly mediated world. These public narratives should not be assumed to tell us anything about individuals' viewpoints or experiences of crime, even when (as we shall see later) media are claiming to be the voice of the individual.

The notion of public narratives is particularly relevant in a mediated world in which there is frequent elision of fiction with apparent reality, as we have seen with the media treatment of women prisoners. The habit of elision is a part of the process of framing public narratives about crime precisely *because* of the all-pervasive nature of media and its images; they are our shared language – whether agreed with or not. This goes beyond being an inventive use of sources for entertainment. Elision of fact and fiction is built into the public narratives within which political and policy debate about crime takes place. So, for example, one BBC TV news (24 July 2004) featured a discussion concerning whether the 1960s were the start of the decline leading to the moral and criminal wasteland which, apparently, some argue that we now inhabit. The anchorman questioned two experts: one (in true debating fashion) for the motion, one against. He turned to the one 'against' and questioned her about social change: surely back then – *Dixon of Dock Green* – when everyone could leave their doors open …? This subtle elision of fiction with current apparent-crisis was just a precursor to a question. Dixon, the famous TV policeman, represents a fictional account of London police in the post-war period. Sydney-Smith (2002) describes the impact of such mythology and iconography:

> Working upon a consolidated sense of the collective memory, the 'Dixon' image is able to transcend the often less than pleasant 'real life' facts of today's policing methods. (p. 2)

It is more, however, than the acceptance or not of myth: it marks, indeed, the shared 'knowledge' of public narratives. That is, the accepted facts and apparent history that make up the story of crime within the public arena. It is shorthand: while we all know it is not *actually* true, we are assumed to know what it means and accept the faux-historical reference to a perceived better time. For public narratives include the virtual media world of meta-crime, in which everything is known but little is actually as it appears.

This fictional–factional questioning on Sunday morning television came in the wake of Prime Minister Tony Blair's announcement that he was starting another campaign against crime (week ending 24 July 2004). This new start was to be based on scrapping the 'liberal consensus' of the 1960s. This second historical shorthand had also featured in the BBC news discussion, and when introduced by the Prime Minister, is an invitation to people to take sides or to declare which side they are on. The historical accuracy of the invitation is of marginal relevance in the meta-history of factional contest. A call to take sides is not just about party politics, but about how the world should be interpreted. 'Framing' of stories refers to the ways in which news media offer not just stories, but perspectives that 'place the events and issues within particular contexts and encourage audiences to understand them in particular ways' (McCullagh, 2002: 25). So, in the example of sex reporting in Northern Ireland, Greer (2003) presents newspapers as offering an invitation to 'decent' people (who could be termed 'people like us') to join in moral condemnation of the wrongdoing 'other' (p. 41). Greer describes this as transcending party politics, and it is this unifying marking of boundaries between the socially good and bad, the 'in' and the 'out', that Peelo and Soothill referred to as the definitional debates inherent in public narratives (2000).

Public narratives, then, can be constructed and debated within a range of shared images; however, this does not mean that criminologists can merge so many issues. So, for example, Potter (2003) argues that there are eleven myths about media violence that need to be unravelled in order to begin to make real sense of violent crime. In his view, there are four groups working from within the interests of their own group to maintain a level of immobility in the public debate around violent crime. Potter's four groups are: the public, producers, policy-makers and researchers. There is much in this thesis that is credible; however, it is hard to discern in reality the levels of homogeneity implied by these groupings, especially 'the public'. This is particularly so given the shift in understanding that the postmodernist paradigm has brought about. Jewkes (2004) succinctly describes the postmodernist view of media entertainment and audience gratification: 'It is the fragmentary, ephemeral and ambiguous that are observed, and pleasure, spectacle, pastiche, parody and irony are the staples of postmodern media output' (p. 26) 'Fragmentation' and pluralism are illustrated by the range of media interwoven with our lives, communicating in different ways with varied audiences, all reading messages in the light of their own worlds.

Further, Jewkes argues that a postmodernist approach problematises the arena of public debate:

> The abandonment of a distinction between information and entertainment raises two problems, however. The first is the threat to meaningful debate that postmodernism seems to imply. A media marketplace based on a pluralist model of ideological struggle may suffice as a forum for debate, but it relies on the public's ability to discriminate between what's true and what is not; between fact and interpretation. (p. 26)

Similarly, Potter points up the difficulties of thinking about social good rather than focusing merely on individual rights and consumption; but this question needs to be thought about, as Jewkes does, within the framework of a varied, pluralist society. Potter is not alone in focusing on the misunderstandings surrounding crime. Felson (1998) bases his analysis of crime on ten fallacies, including the 'dramatic', 'cops-and-courts' and the 'not me' fallacies; and he distinguishes between gaining information from systematic sources as a basis for analysis and our usual sources of the media and personal experience. The social components that shape public narratives, along with Potter's notion of interest groups and myths and Felson's fallacies, need to be carefully disentangled and explored if criminologists are to make meaningful statements about media and crime.

A contested arena: news distortion and impression management

To make sense of the current state of public narratives concerning crime one must recognise that two trends have combined: the escalation of the use of crime events, especially those featuring sex and violence, as infotainment in an increasingly competitive market and impression management as a major political tool in a mediated world.

Infotainment

Infotainment refers to the blurring of entertainment and information. Jewkes has commented that postmodernism 'emphasises the style and packaging of media output in addition to the actual substance of its content' (p. 26). Certainly, entertainment based on the reporting of apparent news information is partly a matter of style which necessarily provides distorted accounts of crime events. Further, Jewkes summarises the view that even news reporting in a competitive market system privileges the sensational, the violent and the highly personalised over 'in-depth political commentary or sustained analysis' (p. 23). This shift towards infotainment as a commonplace is not total or uncontested within the world of journalism: Kovach and Rosenstiel (2001) argue forcefully that traditional journalism is linked to democracy, freedom of the press and the provision of verified information to their fellow citizens, all of which they see threatened by 'the rise of a market-based journalism increasingly divorced from the idea of civic responsibility' (p. 30).

While some elements of the media struggle with a rationalist model of news reporting, television, radio and newspapers depend to some extent on forms of popularity, advertising and sales. Hence, infotainment is the order of the day when attempting to engage popular attention rather than accurate portrayals of daily existence. Infotainment is a form of fiction that takes its departure from real events, but not in the traditional academic sense that assumes fiction to be untruth. Rather, taking a wider view of fiction – as interpretive of the world, as communicative and analytical about lived experience – then, of course, crime news as fiction becomes a more relevant theme to criminologists. The nature, construction, function and text of criminological narratives become more open to analysis.

Distortion

Distortion refers both to the impression conveyed about a particular crime event and to the impression given about the prevalence of particular types of crime. So, for example, in relation to violent crime, Reiner states that the 'proportion of different crimes represented is the inverse of official statistics' (2002: 393). This is reflected in numerous studies, especially in the media treatment of sex and/or violence – particularly homicide (see, for example, Ditton and Duffy, 1983; Greer, 2003; Johnstone et al., 1994; Peelo et al., 2004; Soothill and Walby, 1991; Sorenson et al., 1998).

The reporting of crime is, of necessity, selective. The role of the media is not solely to engage in accuracy and education, and estimating the prevalence of any given crime is fraught with difficulty (see Soothill et al., 2002: 25–35). Newspapers and television do not carry accounts of each and every crime committed within a town, county or country. Journalists' selection criteria, therefore, have been subject to close scrutiny from criminologists, along with the processes by which crime events transmute into items of news. Jewkes (2004) argues that twelve news values and structures underpin journalistic decisions of newsworthiness and these include: sex, violence, conservative ideology, children, simplification, predictability, spectacle, proximity, risk, celebrity, individualism and threshold of importance (see pp. 36–61). Greer (2003) discusses earlier categorisations of the news values that inform newsworthiness decisions (most notably Chibnall, 1977 and Kidd-Hewitt, 1995), but finishes by placing 'spatial and cultural proximity' as an important ingredient in complex mixtures of values, alongside 'personalisation and celebrity, the sense of seriousness and drama' (p. 59) when the newsworthiness of sex crimes is considered.

In a culture of infotainment, it is easy to argue that distortion has little relevance, simply because accurate social accounts are the business of criminologists and sociologists rather than journalists. But these fictive accounts – a part of the jigsaw that makes up public narratives – while *necessarily* based on journalists' selections of newsworthiness, nonetheless help to validate who is included and who is excluded from public concern, whether this is done intentionally or as the side effect of other concerns. Hence we return to a concern about the tension between individual consumption (entertainment) and thinking about the social good. So, for example, research in the US has probed which homicides attract more coverage than others. Johnstone et al. (1994) found that some victims are more likely to be reported than others: murders of African American and Hispanic victims were *less* likely to be reported, while the murders of women and children were *more* likely to be presented. Distortion validates the privileging of some groups over others. Johnstone et al. express their concerns about the social consequences of distorted reporting '… that essentially ignores the economic and social underpinnings of the problem …' and leaves the impression '… that the lives of some groups of Americans are more important than those of others' (1994: 870). Similarly, Greer (2003) comments on the reluctance of newspaper journalists in Northern Ireland to acknowledge the danger to children of incest within the family, preferring the notion of 'stranger-danger' (pp. 144–5).

Impression management

Both political initiatives and media stories depend on popular validation. While impression management and fictionalised crime accounts work at a social level, they take their validation from a battle to be seen as representing the viewpoint of 'ordinary' people. But it is questionable whether one viewpoint can summarise all groups' opinions. So, for example, Peelo et al.'s (2004) study of press representation of homicide illustrates the ways in which there are 'family likenesses' between newspapers, but also subtle differences. Each newspaper produces its own distortion, as some homicides attract some newspapers more than others. Each paper is in conversation with its own readership, making judgements about what will engage them. Competition for the popular voice has intensified during the last thirty years, a period – according to social historians – of noticeable social change (see, for example, Black, 2004; Harris, 2003; Rosen, 2003). Perhaps it is this aspect of the quest for populism that is reflected in Reiner's view that research 'reveals not only that there is more diversity, negotiation and contingency within news organizations than the hegemony model implies, but also in the sources used' (2002: 405).

Garland (2001) has theorised the nature of change in policy and thinking about social order and control that, he argues, has occurred since the 1970s: this has been typified by the emergence of a highly politicised, populist policy-making process which has overturned accepted ways of thinking and previously acknowledged expertise. Hence, Garland argues, a 'highly charged political discourse now surrounds all crime control issues, so that every decision is taken in the glare of publicity and political contention and every mistake becomes a scandal' (p.13). Seen from this perspective, the presentation of crime issues and the development of crime policy are framed as a matter of political advantage against a backdrop that emphasises the drama of crime and criminality. Alongside this political framing of crime, an essential ingredient in the brand of populism described by Garland is the need for both politicians and media people to appear to speak for the rest of the population.

Michael Cockerell (1988), once chief political reporter for the BBC's investigative programme *Panorama*, has charted a parallel process of the growth in importance of television in the lives of British Prime Ministers, from Churchill to Margaret Thatcher. Politics has increasingly become impression management in the television age; indeed, Cockerell argues that in spite of tensions between broadcasters and politicians and in spite of their declared independence, broadcasters 'have sometimes been willing participants in prime ministerial charades made especially for television' (p. xiv). His point was that the actuality of political life and the impressions constructed were quite different. The growing centrality of television as the prime channel for political communication is, in Cockerell's account, an outcome of prime ministerial opportunism as well as that of the broadcasters.

Alongside prime ministerial use of television, Barnett and Gaber (2001) argue that there has been a diminution in political journalists' respect and respectfulness in reporting and questioning of politicians, resulting in greater transparency and accountability (or, at least, accountability to journalists); this has, however, placed journalists in positions of great power in relation to governments and their policies. Hence, Barnett and Gaber argue:

> Politicians now believe, rightly or wrongly, that the media hold the key to electoral success and that any and every technique is permissible in their determination to convey their message – even if those techniques are inimical to the principles of transparency and proper democratic debate. (2001: 136–7).

The role of political impression management (usually referred to as 'spin') has, itself, become a news story. The battle for control of television screens, the tensions and cooperations between politicians and media people has escalated as policy initiatives become suspected of being media gimmicks, and government vies (especially close to elections) with tabloid newspapers to show that they – more than anyone else – are in tune with 'the people'. Downes and Morgan (2002) have, like Garland, described the move to political centre-stage of all matters related to law and order, particularly since 1979:

> … government and Opposition will battle for the high ground as to who best promotes public safety, effective policing, and law enforcement. In reaction, the law and order practitioner associations … will seek to secure party political support for their vested interests, or what they will claim to be the public interest or human rights. (p. 318)

In such a scenario, political success depends on the ability to engage with the rich emotionality surrounding crime, which then becomes a political tool. It is within this contested, populist, public arena that crime and related policies are fought over and, hence, within which public narratives must be deconstructed.

The changing roles of public narratives

The centrality of crime to both the political and media agendas makes important reporting distortions and differentiates the roles of current public narratives from those of previous times. Meanwhile, impression management is a key political tool, and both politicians and media people are locked in battle for the 'hearts and minds' of the rest of the population. The contest for control of media images – that are interwoven with daily life – becomes even more pressing when 'spin' is assumed to be highly influential at all levels of knowledge.

The escalation of competition in media markets and their use of crime have been coupled with a specific form of populism that has crime at its centre, and this coupling has led to a focus on the emotions surrounding crime and criminality. An important ingredient, then, in understanding public narratives is the examination of media expression and exploration of the emotionality surrounding crime. As a site of contest, within which different viewpoints struggle for control of the agenda, a public narrative is integral to managing the emotional reactions that necessarily inform our responses to crime, especially major and serious cases. To make sense of the construction and role of public crime narratives, researchers need to explore the nature of media–audience dialogue, particularly in relation to the rich range of emotionality explored in media content.

Consumption of crime, distancing and emotionality

As we have seen, politicians and journalists *in practice* expect a range of media images to influence popular opinion. However, it is not an intellectual argument alone about crime that is won through public, mediated narratives of crime, but an emotional one. Winning the 'hearts and minds' of the electorate is a different activity in an era of infotainment to, for example, news reporting of the 1950s, and while there remains a lively, analytical genre of political journalism, this is not the bulk of media treatment of crime (plus, however rational, it is a genre that still requires careful analysis by criminologists). At the centre of infotainment is the 'human interest' story with which viewers and readers can easily identify emotionally. The story could be about them or their family, someone they know or, someone such as children and the elderly, people for whom they feel a responsibility.

Distancing

Yet, paradoxically, while media techniques often invite individuals to identify and engage emotionally with a story, this is achieved by objectifying the experiences of actual crime participants, especially crime victims. Further, Reiner (2002) describes how the 'space–time distanciation between criminal cases and their reporting, and the reciprocal feedback of images on practice, are eroding rapidly' (p. 407). Technological develop-ments have resulted in rapid packaging of crime stories ready for consumption, and this immediacy is interwoven with the emotional distancing inherent in objectification. Hence, when examining the emotionality surrounding media representations of crime, one must be aware of the tensions surrounding 'distancing'.

Indeed, Jewkes (2004) has gone further in describing a process of collusion by which we all distance ourselves from the actuality of crime:

> ... the relationship between media and audience in defining the parameters of social (in)tolerance and social control is not only complex, but is one of collusion. To be blunt, crime is constructed and consumed in such a way as to permit the reader, viewer or listener to side-step reality rather than confronting or 'owning up' to it. (p. 201)

Taking this viewpoint, it is possible to go further and argue that, in the act of consumption of crime stories, individuals are taking part in a public narrative that objectifies emotionality, leaving those who *actually* experience crime potentially more distanced and isolated than ever.

Emotionality

In the extensive literature discussing how media representations of crime impact on people, the two emotional states usually discussed are aggression (causing violent behaviour) and fear (for a review of this literature, see Reiner, 2002: 396–402). Criminologists, like others in society, have been much taken with the question of media influence on society, particularly whether media representation of crime provokes a fear of crime. Kidd-Hewitt (1995), for example, has described the media as 'purveyors of fear, consternation and dread' and part of a 'post-modern spectacle' (pp. 18–21). He describes, in particular, television reconstruction of crime to assist in its detection (in Britain the main such programme is called *Crimewatch*) as leading to 'a paradigmatic confusion' in which fact and fiction and fictionalised fact 'all occupy the same pathological universe' (p. 21).

Ditton et al. (2004) illustrate how a range of possible interactions between audiences and media are possible even when fear is seen as the major focus for study; they distinguish between levels of worry and argue that 'the interpretive relevance that people place' on media input is more important than 'the numeric frequency of media consumption' (p. 602). However, emotionality surrounding crime is much richer than that of fear alone (even 'fear' in criminological writing subsumes related emotions such as anxiety, worry, fear). The academic exploration of the wider range of emotionality expressed through and around crime has become associated with cultural criminology. So, for example, Presdee (2000) has emphasised the role of pleasure in crime. In his thesis, the commodification of crime includes the commodification of the emotions surrounding it, including excitement and pleasure. It is these two sets of emotions, he argues, that the media objectify, commodify and then distribute:

> Crime and violence have become objectified and commodified and, as such, much desired whilst being distributed through various forms of media to be pleasurably consumed. (p. 59)

All this consumption of crime, all these attendant emotions, arise without individuals needing to engage personally with acts of illegality.

From a political viewpoint, the role of newspapers in presenting the voice of ordinary individuals with all the human concerns of day-to-day living can feel like an important, liberating development of the media over the last thirty years. But Presdee has warned us to beware of such easy interpretations, for our emotions too are commodified. To explain his view, Presdee calls on the notion of the 'third person' standing outside our reality with whom we can be sociable and share confidences (e.g. a barperson).

> The modern media pretend to be the third brave person of modernity. But in reality we are betrayed as our individual lives and deeply personal identities are commodified and consumed by others. The modern media don't mock *for* us, they mock *at* us. (p. 75 – emphasis in original)

Certainly, people whose lives have brushed against the media as part of their experience of crime report mixed feelings about the process. The media provide police with extensive channels for gathering information. Murders, in particular, have long provided stories for newspapers and now television (Soothill et al., 2002) and families of victims of murder depend on these media to help find killers. This cooperation, then, exposes them to public attention at a time of vulnerability, and they are, albeit fragile, at the heart of an exciting media event. Even when stories are framed to promote the victim perspective, families of murder victims can experience their treatment by representatives of the media as exploitative and insensitive (see, for example, Rock, 1998, especially pp. 83–8; and André Hanscombe's (1996) account of his relationship with the media after the murder of his partner, Rachel Nickell).

Mediated witness

So, criminologists must learn to read the techniques of infotainment more precisely in order to disentangle the emotional underpinnings of a given story. Learning to read images and texts through understanding a producer's techniques is one route to charting how they are trying to engage the audience-readership. For example, 'mediated witness' is the means by which the focus for strong feeling is on the legitimate hurt of victims and through which audiences are invited to identify with victim emotions. In addition to being the unifying call to 'all decent people' of public narratives, the common authorial technique of 'mediated witness' is one by which the audience is invited to take sides in the social commentary which attaches to crimes. For 'mediated witness' aligns the reader emotionally with victimhood; but this *virtual* victimhood must be distinguished from the real experience of actual victims of crime, their families, friends and acquaintances.

One of the chief emotional distinctions between virtual and actual victimhood (in addition to the actuality of experience) is that virtual experience allows us still to be entertained by crime. Major crime touches us all as members of the community yet provides us, as individual consumers, with a commodity that is a source of entertainment, thrills and fear.

Moral panics

The traditional theoretical framework in criminology within which media engagement with emotive, social construction of crime events is usually examined is that of 'moral panics'. Micro-level analysis of media representations, illustrated by 'mediated witness', is set against a macro-level analysis of the socio-political and historical context. As an applied subject, criminology is grounded in the events that occur within society, yet as an academic study we place findings within the framework of an existing theoretical framework. 'Moral panics' was a phrase and concept coined in the 1970s (Cohen, 1972/2002) which aptly and accurately caught the moment in its description of media responses particularly to youth behaviour. The role of distortion and moral outrage in amplifying deviance and reinforcing marginality (especially in relation to 'mods and rockers') was drawn with outstanding social insight. However, since then the phrase has been applied to a range of matters of public concern (see Thompson, 1998), and one must question whether all emotive, sensational phenomena that cause public concern (whether or not stirred through media coverage) should automatically be called 'moral panics'.

Given that society changes, existing theoretical frameworks can become a burden rather than aiding explanation and understanding of current crime phenomena. One further danger with a successful theoretical framework, such as 'moral panics', is that it can be used as shorthand whereby a phenomenon is summarised and dismissed. We are then stopped from examining any deeper when we should be working to provide a broader palette, a wider range of interpretive devices. Emotionality, for example, is assumed here to be a rich response to human life, and as such it requires detailed and careful exploration rather than rapid dispatching as 'moral panic'.

Jewkes (2004) has well summarised the continued importance of 'moral panics' as an analytic device (pp. 64–86) as well as the problems attached to the concept. She explains that its importance remains in explaining how media can amplify relatively ordinary, albeit deviant, phenomena (to an extent that demonises marginal groups, especially youth subcultures), tapping into what may be existing anxieties within its audiences, so helping to construct social margins and deviancy in a spiral of highly affective campaigning. However, not all emotive media campaigns – even though they meet these criteria – constitute the short-term feeding frenzy of 'media panics'; not all media engagement in attempting to define social consensus or boundaries is so intense or short-lived. Further, in an age of infotainment, sensational, personalised reporting is the means by which media commonly engage audiences and readers through the use of emotional identification, and there is a much wider range of possible emotions than the monochromatic picture implied by use of 'panic' alone.

There is a danger, too, that when academics overstate the emotional response of media audiences as 'panic', they can sound disdainful of what could, from other vantage points, be acknowledged as legitimate public concerns. Further, when criticising the 'moral' component of media interest (rather than just the 'panic'), academic writing can appear to question the right of the media and public to concern themselves with social values.

The media provide the means for public debate in ways unimagined even one hundred years ago, so the contest for control of the 'moral' or social control agenda is contested energetically within a public arena almost daily. A newsworthy crime issue will invariably be surrounded by a social or moral commentary (it is a part of the invitation to join the 'decent' people who share your viewpoint). Having limited conceptual frameworks for describing this public contest means that we often need to use the 'moral' in 'moral panics' even when the whole 'moral panic' concept is inappropriate. 'Moral panics' originally pointed the way for criminologists in showing the need to work at both the social and affective levels when interpreting media impact on the social construction of crime.

But *additional* approaches are often possible and, with a changing world, *wider* constructs for interpretation are needed. 'Public narrative' is both an historical artefact and a heuristic that helps to explore the public arena within which crime is represented, defined and contested, including its emotional aspects, over time. It refers to a slower, more commonplace and cumulative process occurring over a longer time period than is the case with 'moral panics'.

Conclusion

Public narratives are the shared stories by which societies contest and relate a public account of, in this instance, crime. For criminologists they are the means by which, given the shift in thinking about mediated matter that has resulted from the development of a postmodern perspective, we can explore the shared, social arena in a world that is otherwise perceived as fragmented and as primarily about individualised consumption. How is the public agenda contested and how is it controlled in a world apparently subject not to group identity but to myriad choices for individual consumption? Where there is a plethora of media choices attempting to echo the individual viewpoint, then the location and processes of control and power are not as overt and clear-cut as they were in the 1950s and 1960s. Students of criminology must look more closely to disentangle how crime is socially constructed in a mediated world.

Abercrombie et al. (2000) describe sociological discussions of media and society as containing two contrasting views – that media coherently promote the views of the powerful to an uncritical audience and that the media represent a variety of views and 'that the audience is capable of reacting critically' (p. 368). They themselves take the view '... that members of the audience are knowledgeable about the media and are capable of being critical about what they watch, read and hear' (p. 368). It is in the interaction between audiences and media that the complexity of public narratives lives, and they are shaped in a society in which crime is a highly politicised, contested topic at the heart of power struggles.

We have already noted that Peelo et al. (2004) observed differences in newspapers' selection of murder stories. In a competitive market, media outlets (especially television and newspapers) want to be the legitimate voice of their audience, to communicate and to find their audiences in agreement with their message. This does not mean that we can assume that what is in the public arena is public opinion, or that an acknowledged public narrative is an exact match with individual experience and belief about crime. Populism, of itself, does not equal control of people's minds. Ditton et al. (2004) have, for example, illustrated how individual responses to media representations of crime can be explained by how those representations interact with a person's history and outlook. While readerships and audiences may acknowledge the power of particular public narratives, we do not know the extent to which these may interact with individual viewpoints.

So criminologists need to question the media whenever there appears to be an illusion of social homogeneity or a sense of knowledge and understanding. There is a need to challenge simplistic models of media effects or when audiences are presented as passive or as easily subject to media conspiracy. Criminologists need to move beyond seeing fear as the only affective issue and understand at a micro-level how media representations of crime are inviting audiences to respond. Public narratives are cumulative and historical (but not necessarily historically informed), so one needs to be alert to references to earlier crimes and crime issues as a part of inviting audiences to take sides in a wider social commentary surrounding a specific current event.

The concept of 'moral panics' was originally devised at a different point in time, where choices for audiences were fewer and the interaction between audiences and media representations of crime (especially via television) were also different. The expectation that social consensus could be easily defined was more commonplace. But, since then, the main impact of the postmodernist paradigm shift on thinking about media has been to oblige criminologists to face up to the fragmented, pluralist nature of both the media and their audiences. However, while individual choice and consumption is of primary concern within this paradigm, it should not prevent us from recognising the continued presence of contest for control of the public agenda. It is easy to fall into the trap of believing that there is no public arena at all, hence believing that there is no power struggle relating to social control, and that there is no public or social impact on the construction of crime. The concept of a public narrative is one that provides a framework for *starting* to analyse how the public contest for social control meets individual consumption of media representations of crime within a pluralistic, more fragmented world.

Chapter 3

Racing to conclusions: thinking sociologically about police race relations

Simon Holdaway

Introduction

Criminological research often poses ethical questions. 'Justice', 'fairness', 'punishment' and many other concepts that are commonplace in criminological debate have clear ethical dimensions. Research about police race relations poses ethical questions sharply. Racism is a denial of what we regard as 'human'; discrimination on the criteria of race and/or ethnicity is unjust and unfair. We are opposed to racism. Criminological evidence can support our objection. Policies that lead to racial discrimination should be changed, informed by evidence from criminology.

If only the world was so simple. Research evidence is often ambiguous, and necessarily so. The link between policy and research findings is not straightforward. Ethics are relevant to but cannot alone drive the design of criminological research and the interpretation of data. Criminology is not just about changing the world. All criminological research is based on theoretical assumptions of direct relevance to policy and other areas of reform.

In this chapter about an aspect of police race relations, it is argued that reform is likely to flounder without a critical awareness of the theoretical assumptions informing research. Students of criminology must be theoreticians before they can be commentators on societal and policy reform – a stance not all criminology students relish.

A contemporary perspective

There was a difficult moment during Monday's MA Criminology class. The students had read extracts from George Herbert Mead's 'Mind, Self and Society', in which he introduces his conceptualisation of 'the self', and considered its implications for criminological research (Mead, 1934). My MA module is entitled 'The Cultures of Criminology', concerned with understanding how all criminological perspectives and 'lay' commentaries about crime are founded upon explicit or implicit theoretical assumptions. Each perspective includes a philosophical anthropology, a view about human nature, about how we understand the world around us, and related views about how evidence to support our understanding should be gathered.

The trouble is that criminologists and other commentators rarely stand back to reflect on these assumptions. My aim is to encourage and teach budding criminologists to consider accounts of crime and related subjects – academic, media-based, conversational or any other commentary, it does not matter – and probe beneath their surface to identify the theoretical assumptions underpinning the arguments presented. Our critical, analytical powers must surely be developed and honed by such an approach. It helps us develop better policy and practice.

Last Monday, a student mustered the courage to ask, 'What's the relevance of all this?' meaning, 'What has this got to do with the "real world", with changing it?' A discernible 'Mmm, we agree' hummed around the class. My recollection was that we had discussed this important question during the first teaching session considering, for example, how unquestioned, taken-for-granted assumptions about human nature, about the veracity of supporting evidence, about the reasoning that relates evidence to policy prescriptions, and about ethical consistency lead to the failure of policy. Our earlier discussion was obviously unfinished. There was a strong (implicit now becoming explicit) view in the class that criminology is or should be an academic subject about understanding the world of crime, offenders and offending, and their institutions, *in order to change them*, presumably for the better, whatever that means. The emphasis should be on changing the world. There is a strong moral imperative to adopt that clear stance.

Having started my working life as a police officer, studied as a mature student and, over a good number of years, undertaken research that has tried to inform national policy, I find questions like the one posed legitimately last Monday concerning (Holdaway, 1991; Holdaway et al., 2001). It is, simply, disappointing that theoretical questions are viewed increasingly as arcane, somehow separated from the 'real world'. Even more disturbing is that many criminologists around the world would agree with my MA students!

Arguments about the place of the academy in contemporary society apart, criminology should not just be about applied questions, about evaluating policy and practice to improve one or the other. Much of contemporary criminological research, however, is undertaken on the (wrong) assumption that it is properly atheoretical. Technical questions about research methods are admitted. Unquestioned assumptions about the social context within which criminological research questions arise are neglected. Current policy and practice calls the tune of much contemporary criminology, which is concerned with 'relevance' and, in the latest jargon, 'what works' (browse this web site for information about this perspective: http://www.crimereduction.gov.uk/cpindex.htm).

I want to argue that criminology should be about changing the world beyond the academy. In equal and greater measure, however, I want to argue that it is about understanding that same world through a radical questioning of the assumptions that inform everyday discourse about and action in the worlds of crime, offending, offenders and the institutions related to them, including current policy and practice. We need to foster a 'criminological imagination', placing contemporary criminological research within a wider context than the immediacy of policy and practice, while not distancing it wholly from them (Mills, 1959).

Race and ethnicity

Race and ethnic relations is one area of criminological research that demonstrates well the need for a reflective, criminological imagination. People are categorised by others as members of races. We ascribe people to membership of races, usually identified by some combination of skin colour, physiological characteristics and genetic background. In fact, such categorisation by criteria drawn from biology, physiology or genetics is unsupported by scientific evidence. The scientific consensus is that human beings cannot be divided into membership of distinct biological races. We share inherited differences as human beings but they are continuous, not a set of separate, distinct packages of traits.

This, however, does not mean that 'races' do not exist and are therefore unimportant. People talk about races; they identify themselves with and act personally and collectively as members of a race; they go to war in the name of their race and fight members of another race; and they commit genocide to cleanse the world of a particular race. 'Races' might not be biologically distinct but they are *socially constructed* and, clearly, very powerful when mobilised (Banton, 1987; Miles, 1989). 'Races' exist as social constructions, which means that criminologists should be sceptical of any claims people make about their impact on crime and offending but nevertheless regard them as real, with effects on others' actions. Without doubt, races have a documented impact on the social world, including the world of crime and its institutions (Bowling and Phillips, 2000).

Racism

When an association is made between behaviour and membership of a race, we find 'racism'. The idea that being black and therefore naturally criminal, being Asian and naturally devious, being white English and naturally conservative and, crucially, acting on the basis on the association between biology and behaviour is 'racism'. The key to this thinking and acting is founded upon a direct association between biology/genetics and action.

A number of scholars have recently extended the notion of racism. Advocates of the 'new racism' argue that the association between biology/genetics and behaviour is not the only form in which racism is constructed (Barker, 1981; Hall, 1992; Cohen, 1993). Race-thinking and action – racism – can also be based on an association between culture and behaviour. Some suggest, for example, that Asians have a different culture from us, associated with Islam and therefore are likely to be political terrorists, that black British youth are immersed in an innate culture of violence and therefore are naturally violent. Cultures are not unrelated to human action but affording them a primordial status and relating them directly to explain behaviour is, so the argument runs, racist. The direct association between culture and behaving in a particular way because one is a member of a culturally defined group is a form of racism, the new racism.

You should consider the strengths and weaknesses of these arguments that extend the concept of racism because, as some have argued, it could be concluded that they render it redundant, stretched to its limit to encompass very different criteria. You might as well interpret any differentiation between ethnic minority groups within criminal justice institutions as racism.

Ethnicity

Ethnicity is distinct from race. Ethnicity is the concept used to describe our membership of an ethnic group. We are categorised into races by others but ascribed (by ourselves) to membership of an ethnic group, usually identifying a common heritage of culture, occupancy of land and/or other characteristics to secure our claim (Jenkins, 1994, 1997). Ethnicity is subjective, based on actors' definitions and on the social context in which people claim a common heritage, culture, or some other identification. This allows people to regard themselves as members of a particular ethnic group, which can be an ethnic majority – white people in England, for example – or an ethnic minority. Importantly, membership of an ethnic group can be variable. I can regard myself as English in one context and Asian in another (Barth, 1969). There is nothing fixed about ethnicity. Black English people may regard themselves increasingly as members of an ethnic minority if they are the subjects of over-policing by being stopped and searched disproportionately. They perhaps feel an enhanced individual and collective identity in this context but not within their multi-ethnic workplace, where they identify with the ethnic majority.

One implication of this view is that we should understand processes and relationships that lead to categorisations and ascriptions of race and ethnicity, and the contexts in which they are pertinent. We will see later that research about the police use of stop and search powers has tended to be concerned with measuring their differential use. It has not focused upon processes and relationships that have led to the stop and searches measured and analysed statistically to reveal disproportionality. My criticism of this type of research is its failure to reflect on the analytical status of 'race' as a social construction and, therefore, its inability to be the basis of policy reform.

It is not difficult to recognise a moral dimension when criminological research reveals that stop and search powers are being used to sustain racial discrimination. The disproportionate use of stop and search powers by the police on members of some ethnic groups is not only based on erroneous criteria influencing officers' use of discretion but, importantly, on the exercise of injustice. And when criminologists identify injustice, they surely cannot stand back from it? There is an imperative to change the world, to work for justice. It is not sufficient to undertake research that identifies injustice – criminology has to go further and seek change.

I agree and disagree with this view about the moral context of criminological research. No, we cannot stand back from the ethical and related political implications of our research. We can choose to find ways to lobby for and create change if we have a mind to do so. However, it is grandiose to think that research findings and related criminological arguments alone can lead to significant change. The relationship between research and policy is notoriously slight (Pawson and Tilley, 1997).

I also think that we need to place ethical questions in their proper research place, by which I mean that ethical imperatives should not be the tail that wags the researching dog. If members of one ethnic minority group are found to have been stopped and searched in disproportionate numbers when compared to those from, say, an ethnic majority in a population, we cannot immediately claim to have identified a moral imperative for criminologists to turn injustice to justice. As we will see later, there may be all sorts of good reasons determined by criminological research to explain apparent injustice.

Ethics cannot depend on provisional research findings for their veracity. The practice of criminological research, including data analysis and dissemination, cannot be driven by ethics alone. Research may challenge ethics but need to be regarded as provisional. Some findings may beg the revision of ethical principles, however.

Stop and search

The disproportionate police use of stop and search powers against ethnic minorities has been a persistent theme of criminological research, and one that has raised questions about the extent to which the police use their powers ethically (Smith, 1997; Tonry, 1997; Rowe, 2004). The Police and Criminal Evidence Act (PACE) 1984 introduced rules governing police discretion when using a new power to stop and search people suspected of crime, replacing the greater freedom afforded by a power to stop suspected persons under the 1824 Vagrancy Act. Data to establish any police bias in the use of the 1824 Act was patchy, to say the least. They were simply not collected routinely. Jock Young and John Lea, however, estimated the Act was the statute under which 42 per cent of the arrests of black people were made, suggesting that a very widely drawn and interpreted police power was being used disproportionately against black people (Lea and Young, 1984). More precise data were required if their conclusion was to be given adequate evidential weight.

More carefully ordered data about stop and search were gathered during a large, early 1980s study of policing (Smith, 1986). It was found that, when on foot, blacks were four times more likely to be stopped than people from other ethnic groups; 49 per cent of people of West Indian backgrounds who owned or had the regular use of a vehicle said they had been stopped by the police (Smith, 1986: 249–55). The criteria used to stop seemed to extend beyond 'suspicion of committing an offence', ranging from demeanour to driving a BMW. This study drew some public and, importantly, police and Home Office attention to the improper use of discretion by officers and, in time, it was decided that more careful government monitoring was required.

The opportunity to monitor more rigorously the police use of use of stop and search powers came with the Police and Criminal Evidence Act (PACE) in 1984, but progress towards national monitoring was slow. In 1993, Her Majesty's Inspector of Constabulary required all police forces to document the ethnic origin of people stopped. The categories for data collection were twofold, white and ethnic minorities, meaning that it was not possible to differentiate the number of stops between or within ethnic minority groups. Analysis of the first year's figures – 1994/5 – showed that ethnic minorities were four times more likely to be stopped than white people (per thousand within the population) but, and this is an important point, ethnic minorities did not comprise a similar proportion of the national population. The indication was that the police were discriminating against ethnic minorities when using their power to stop and search (Rowe, 2004).

These kinds of findings have persisted for a considerable time. The last Home Office data, for example, drew the following comment from the Steering Group that is overseeing the implementation of major changes recommended by the Lawrence Inquiry (Home Office, 2003). They put it that the figures

> ... show a percentage increase of minority ethnic people being stopped and searched. Also, the 2001/02 figures showed that black people were eight times more likely to be stopped and searched than white people. This was a rise from five times more likely in 1999/2000 and seven times more likely in 2000/01. There is a real need to understand what exactly lies behind these statistics. (p. 4)

The Home Office statement makes evidence of a disproportionate use of stop and search powers seem compelling. There is real concern about the figures, with the Association of Chief Police Officers having a standing committee to monitor data and advocate new approaches, regular Home Office monitoring and publication of data analysis, Her Majesty's Inspectorate of Constabulary undertaking regular thematic inspections of race relations and related aspects of policing, and a watchful media eye ready to publicise official and other reports (Her Majesty's Inspectorate of Constabulary, 1992; Her Majesty's Inspector of Constabulary, 1995; Her Majesty's Inspectorate of Constabulary, 1996, 1997, 1999; Home Office, 2003). To argue that these developments are a sham, shielding a deliberate, covert racism is not sufficient.

We need to read the above quotation again, however, noting the last sentence: 'There is a real need to understand what exactly lies behind these statistics.' Data do not speak for themselves; research to understand the statistics is needed. One implication is that you cannot make ethical judgements on their basis alone; another is that criminological research can demonstrate a disproportionate use of stop and search figures but, and this is a crucial point, it has to go much further than a consideration of the raw data, which is a starting rather than an end point of academic understanding and of policy reform.

This point can be made as strongly to many criminologists as it can to anyone else commenting on stop and search. Research has been dominated by recognition of the problems of using data collected by the police and the more technical aspects of data analysis, but remains theoretically ignorant (Holdaway, 1997b). The basic problem is that research has been concerned with the outcomes of police action. Criminologists have focused upon the act of a police officer stopping and searching a person, and have done so within a limited analytical framework. The basic questions have been, 'How many black, Asian, white (and so one could go on) people have been stopped and searched by officers?' 'Does the analysis demonstrate a disproportionate number of stops of members of an ethnic group when compared to their number in the general population?'

Recognising the limitations of recorded statistics, further related questions have also been asked, and they will be discussed soon. However, as George Herbert Mead reminds us, outcomes are the endpoint of a process of decision-making about racialised categorisations and ascriptions, and about associated relationships that need to be understood. Criminologists have been interested mainly in the outcomes of a *process* of thought in which a police officer decides to stop and search a black person rather than a white person, for example. Criminologists should be as and, in my view, more interested in the process of decision-making and the context within which it is formed, not least if they want to change a process of police thinking and acting that leads to the differential outcomes documented.

Stop and search – explanations

In this section of the chapter, a range of factors that criminologists have thought might explain the disproportionate use of stop and search will be considered. There has been a consideration of the role of demographics, for example. Throughout the 1980s and 1990s, the age range of the black population in Britain was and to some extent remains skewed towards the younger end, meaning that in relative terms more stops of black people could be expected (Stevens and Willis, 1979). Males aged 15–24 commit more crime than those from other age groups, and it is therefore reasonable to expect men who come within this age range, including those from minority ethnic groups, to be stopped more frequently than those outside it. Age may therefore be a more important criterion than ethnicity for the use of stop powers. Studies that have looked at this factor have concluded that some of the differential use of stop and search can be explained by demographics, but by no means all of it.

Another factor is the stop rate rather than the base figures for the number of stops undertaken. Early research by the Policy Studies Institute (PSI) team, for example, found that the average number of stops per year was much higher for black youth than for their white peers, with an average of 5.06 stops for the former compared with 1.94 for the latter (Smith, 1997). Black youth were on the receiving end of repeated police interventions, with a police 'strike rate' of an arrest from stops of 1 in 12. The PSI team concluded that this was 'justified in the sense that an equal proportion of stops of the two groups produce a result' (Smith, 1997: 106) – which seems to stretch the point about the just use of stop and search to near breaking point!

A rather different intervention was made by Tony Jefferson when he argued that, on the basis of an analysis of stop and search in Leeds, social class is an important factor when considering where and when black people are stopped (Jefferson and Walker, 1993). He found that the black rate for stop and search was highest only in areas with low concentrations of blacks and Asians in the population. Younger whites had the highest rates in poorer areas, where the majority of blacks and Asians lived. Several factors could explain these findings (see Holdaway, 1996: 88 for description of them); the main point was that being black and 'out of place and out of class' in an area with a significant white population seemed to figure in the police use of their stop powers. Being white and working class in a middle-class white area would similarly attract disproportionate police attention.

The other explanator that has to be considered is one that might well be encountered frequently in everyday discussion of the policing of black people. Black people are stopped more frequently because they commit more crime. Criminologists began arguing about this in the early 1980s, and did so in pretty raw terms – gradually taking into account a range of factors related to what might be called the 'black (and the white) crime rate' (Holdaway, 1996). It is by no means possible, however, to explain all disparity by arrests and recorded offences in these terms. An element of police discrimination remains, expressed in statistical terms – so much is due to police factors, so much to crime committed, while neglecting to give research attention to processes that lead to the particular outcomes measured .

John Lea and Jock Young responded to this debate from a rather different standpoint (Lea and Young, 1982, 1984). Young was concerned about the polarised terms in which it was conducted. One side argued that the disproportionate stop and search rate was the result of a higher crime rate among black youths. There should be no surprise at the differential findings, no moral denigration of the police. The reply from the other side of the debate was that police discretion was the sole, explanatory factor of relevance. Police racism explained everything (Gilroy, 1982).

Young pointed out that secure evidence indicated higher rates of unemployment, while educational achievement and other major indicators of life chances were disproportionately concentrated among some ethnic minorities. These disadvantages can be associated with higher crime rates within groups affected by them than those that are not. Black youths are disadvantaged when compared to white youths and therefore *some*, not all, are likely to commit a disproportionate amount of crime. The notion of police racism as the sole factor explaining differential stop rates is inadequate.

Further, Young argued that at the time this argument was raging, Asian youths were stopped disproportionately less than would be expected given their number in the general population. If the police were described as 'racist', they could be expected to stop and search a greater number of Asian youths. The lower number of stops for Asians, however, suggests the exercise of positive discrimination by the police, which is hardly consistent with the notion of racism.

The final factor to mention, and one recently proposed, is that the definition of inequity used to interpret research findings is inappropriate. Home Office and, more recently, independent research has not compared stop and search statistics to the relative proportions of ethnic minorities in the general population. The underpinning assumption of this research is that justice lies in a generally proportionate relationship between the size of the ethnic majority and of ethnic minorities in the general population, and the number of stop and searches made on their respective members, taking into account age profiles and related factors of relevance.

A much more adequate basis for assessing equity is the population available to stop in public places. Police officers cannot stop and search most of the ethnic minority populations in the UK, who are at home, at work and in other private places and therefore not available for police attention. In a recent paper, Stenson and colleagues have taken this stance, using measures of the population of ethnic majority and ethnic minority people on the streets in the Thames Valley police area (Waddington, Stenson and Don, 2004).

Moving on

All of this research is important for our understanding of the policing of ethnic minorities in contemporary UK but it is not adequate, and for one basic reason. Race is a social construction rather than a 'fact' that can be measured by stop and search statistics; an outcome of social processes of decisions and related actions that lead a police officer to understand an aspect of police work as one in which race/ethnicity is present (Holdaway, 1997a, 1997b). All the factors mentioned so far have to be taken into consideration when trying to understand stop and search, but the overriding theoretical lens through which they should be viewed is one comprising the social construction of race (Omi and Winant, 1994).

Outcome research signals us to the general framework of thought within which officers exercise their stop and search powers. But it does not explain why they use their powers in a particular way, to engage in processes that lead to the outcomes documented. We have to draw upon the criminological imagination to move on. To do this means considering two contexts of relevance to the police – the institutional and the societal.

When I refer to the institutional context I mean routine ways of thinking and acting that are taken for granted within a particular realm of social life, here the police service (Jenkins, 1996; Holdaway, 1999). Institutions are robust and resist change, and therefore persist over time. Institutions are not monochrome. Different ideas that are not always in harmony persist within the one institution. For example, contemporary chief constables' ideas about stop and search may be rather different from and in conflict with those of their workforce. We know from research completed over a long period, however, that the occupational culture, which is the repository of ideas and related actions of primary reference for officers, is a powerhouse of ideas that, if not overtly tolerant of and expressive of directly racist ideas, has features that can foster discrimination on the grounds of ethnicity (Chan, 1997; Holdaway, 1997a, 1997b). These ideas have persisted and informed police action over decades – they have been institutionalised.

Police thinking, the way in which officers look out upon the world within the context of their work, tends to be categorical. Using police-related criteria, people are differentiated into membership of clearly defined groups, including ethnic groups. Stereotyping, especially racialised stereotyping, is amenable within this context (Holdaway, 1997a, 1997b). A wide gap between the dictates of policy and practice can exist within the context of police work where discretion is increased the further one goes down the chain of command (Skolnick 1966).

This context – and research supports the view – is one within which notions of race can influence action and the ways in which the stop and search power is used. The occupational culture is not just a repository of discourse but one combining ideas and actions. It includes what officers take for granted about the world and ideas and actions they do not question, including ideas and actions about how they should police ethnic minorities. We therefore need to place differential stop and search outcomes within the context of an analysis of the occupational culture of policing, keeping racialised aspects of the culture at the forefront of attention.

Taking these ideas into account, research can move from a concern with outcomes to consideration of officers' taken-for-granted assumptions that lead them to stop more black than white youths. We begin to understand more clearly processes and relationships leading to the outcomes that are usually analysed. Race and ethnicity are constructed through taken-for-granted police ideas and actions that, as the Lawrence Steering Group put it, 'lie behind the figures'.

Occupational cultures are distinct but cannot be separated entirely from the wider social structure within which they are set. This is a further, related context into which police use of stop and search should be placed. There are deep fissures of racial prejudice and discrimination running through contemporary UK society, and negative views about ethnic minorities have been documented among the police. Clearly, there is a relationship between these views and more generally held ideas about ethnic minorities in contemporary Britain. An analysis which suggests that a racist society equals a racist police analysis will not hold. We need to understand the particular relationships between racialised inequalities and disadvantage lodged within the social order and their impact upon policing.

Change

A number of important changes that may have an impact on the police use of stop and search powers are in train. Two of them come from within constabularies where chief officers are demonstrating an awareness of the difficulties the disproportionate use of stop and search are creating for their constabularies and where black police associations are developing apace.

Black police associations

We will consider black police associations (BPAs) first. Virtually all the 43 constabularies of England and Wales have established a BPA, which represents their ethnic minority officers. Recent research has found that associations' officials have a seat at important policy committees, significantly those concerned with aspects of police race relations. One of their key concerns is stop and search; another is the eradication of racism from their working environment. The associations work in many different ways but, generally, they have contributed significantly to the reduction of openly racist language and other forms of marginalisation within the police workforce.

My point is that BPAs are not the sole answer to the problems of stop and search but, importantly, they have introduced some new dimensions to considerations within constabularies. Disparities of stop and search have been personalised in the sense that, when stop and search is discussed, black police officers stress that the recorded statistics refer to people like them; if they or their relatives they were on the streets, they would be stopped simply because they are members of an ethnic minority and for no other reason.

From this perspective, a consequence of policing on the streets becomes more than an operational problem affecting a group 'out there'. Stop and search requires action because it not only has an impact on race relations beyond constabulary boundaries but also resonates within them, and personally in the lives of individual officers. Committee and other discussions within constabularies, including those between rank and file staff from the ethnic minorities and the ethnic majority within the workforce, cannot be dismissed as unimportant or without consequence. If it is known that officers are stopping members of ethnic minorities disproportionately, it is now likely that a BPA will raise the matter with a senior officer on behalf of all ethnic minorities within the constabulary, placing it within more general discussion about stop and search and moving the terms of discussion from outcomes to the processes that led to them.

A further consequence of BPAs is the identification of the occupational culture as a key feature of a reform programme. This was made clear in the evidence of Inspector Paul Wilson, then Chair of the Metropolitan Police BPA, to the Lawrence Inquiry. He put it that:

> … we should not underestimate the occupational culture within the police service as being a primary source of institutional racism in the way that we differentially treat black people … I say we because there is a marked difference between black and white in the force essentially. We are all consumed by this occupational culture. Some of us may think we rise above it on some occasions, but, generally speaking, we tend to conform to the norms of this occupational culture, which we say is all-powerful in shaping our views and perceptions of a particular community. (Macpherson, 1999: 25)

From this perspective, stop and search, and all other aspects of police race relations, are not viewed as discrete problems but have a relationship to the occupational culture. Particular reforms depend upon a more general reform. Wilson's perspective was identified more widely during a study of BPAs I completed recently, meaning that there are now representative associations within UK constabularies that are making a connection between the particular and the general, tracing particular statistical patterns of stop and search to, in the Lawrence Steering Group's words, 'what lies behind them'.

Lastly, a number of BPAs have developed important links with ethnic minority communities living in their constabulary areas. They act as a conduit of communication about policy and needed reform, with benefits to both senior officers and local communities. Black officers, for example, can speak personally about the effects of inappropriate patterns of stop and search, emphasise that they are pressing for reform within their constabulary, and bring to the committee table important information about stop and search (and other matters) gleaned from members of minority groups.

Chief officers

Research conducted ten years ago documented complacency and a lack of understanding about race relations among chief constables and other senior police ranks (Holdaway, 1991). This situation has now changed and there is a marked determination among chief officers, working through their Association of Chief Police Officers (ACPO), to develop new policies and practices to tackle disparities in the use of stop and search. The Lawrence Inquiry was one influence on this change. After the publication of the Lawrence Report, John Newing, then Chair of the Association of Chief Police Officers and Chief Constable of Derbyshire, accepted that 'institutional racism' was a major problem for the police service. Other chief constables, the Chief Constable of Greater Manchester, for example, followed his lead, stating clearly that their constabulary was institutionally racist (Rowe, 2004: 155).

Recognition of a problem is not the same as a concerted action to deal with it. Lawrence brought into public view the problems of police race relations and Home Office circulars required consideration of new policies. We have seen that recent figures for stop and search, however, do not reveal significant change. Something more is required, and this has been provided from outwith constabularies through the televising of *The Secret Policeman* in 2004. The programme, which was filmed covertly, showed a trainee officer at Bruche Police Training Centre boasting about issuing ethnic minority motorists with fixed penalty tickets when he would allow white motorists to get away with their offences. Another trainee was seen wearing a Ku Klux Klan type hood. He was heard to say that he would like to kill Asians and 'bury them under the train tracks'. Perhaps most seriously for chief constables who had been working hard to improve race relations within their constabularies, another recruit said he was partly motivated to join the police because he knew it was a racist organisation. Here, he could 'look after his own'. What, now, was the status of race relations policies and statements? How could ethnic minorities put their wholehearted confidence in any constabulary?

The *Secret Policeman* was not centrally concerned with stop and search but it sent clear messages to the police service and government about all aspects of race relations. ACPO established a strong review of race relations policy, which is now reporting to their central executive. A central aim of the review is concerned with chief constables following a policy that renders all race policies open to monitoring according to a standard assessment template. The policies and means of making them accountable will be placed within the public domain. The expectation is that stop and search figures will be analysed routinely using a standard template.

On the ground, policies that require officers to explain more fully to supervisory staff why they stopped particular people and a more careful targeting of the use of the power through the use of what police call 'intelligence', meaning data about crime in localities and suspected offenders, are more fully in evidence (Bland et al., 2000). This means that some constabularies are trying to limit the general use of stop and search, confining it to geographical areas identified through an analysis of local crime and related data. The aim is that the geographical, indiscriminate use of stop and search will be curbed, and its disproportionate use against ethnic minorities reduced significantly.

The outcomes of these types of schemes are not yet known. Clearly, the statistics show that the publication of the Lawrence report and related Home Office guidance was not sufficient to change long-standing practices. The gap between written policy and policy as it is implemented by officers using their discretion on the streets has been noted over decades of research (Manning, 1977; Holdaway, 1983; Chatterton, 1992). That position is not going to change in the short term. The point is that there is now a new awareness and determination among chief constables and other officers, many of whom are fully aware of the criminological research literature about stop and search, to change the current situation.

Conclusions

'Race' is a social construct. This is the first and last point I want to emphasise strongly in this chapter. If we do not theorise 'race' adequately, we will not be able to understand how it is articulated by police officers as they stop and search people on the streets. Further, if we do not theorise it adequately, we will be unable to undertake reform to create justice and fairness from injustice and unfairness. 'Race' is a social construct.

Criminological research about the police use of stop and search powers has been overwhelmingly concerned with analysing their disproportionate use against some ethnic minorities. Data about the number of stop and search incidents have been analysed and identified patterns of racial discrimination. These analyses, however, have not been straightforward because a host of other factors, e.g. the age profile of an ethnic minority population, could skew the figures.

Further, the statistical analyses of stop and search should be regarded as a starting point rather than an endpoint of criminological research. They inform us about the populations subjected to stop and search powers but not why officers have made decisions to stop *these* rather than *those* people. Research about outcomes has taken priority over processes that lead to the outcomes analysed.

An explanation of the police use of stop and search powers therefore has to be based on a theoretical foundation that places the construction of race in a central place. How can we change the world if we discover that black youths are stopped disproportionately? By assuming that officers will change their behaviour if they are told about rational findings from criminological research? I think not. The analysis of outcomes requires us to trace the origins of myriad ideas, beliefs and related actions that form processes leading to discriminatory outcomes. Crucially, students of criminology need to be aware of the changing contexts within which social processes are moulded and articulated, and there are significant changes in the area of research discussed. When the Lawrence Monitoring Group stated, 'There is a real need to understand what exactly lies behind these statistics', they were begging rather more than the statistical analyses that had identified the disproportionate use of stop and search powers. They were requiring us to be theoreticians.

Chapter 4

Inequality and crime

Chris Grover

Introduction

This chapter argues that if criminology is serious about addressing crime it must take as its starting point relationships between inequality and crime. In particular, it argues that criminology needs to be as much about analyses of social justice and social policy as it is about criminal justice and criminal justice policy. In doing this, I focus upon the nature and extent of inequalities in contemporary society and evidence of relationships between crime and inequality.

The chapter also highlights the common ground between criminology and social policy by focusing upon the ways in which crime and social policy are structured through similar concerns with personal responsibility. By focusing upon the contradictions of particularly income maintenance and labour market policy, I demonstrate that such policies can exacerbate, rather than alleviate, inequalities.

The Prison Reform Trust (cited in Cook, 1997: 87) has found that 12 per cent of convicted and 17 per cent of remand prisoners were homeless at the time of their imprisonment and that nearly half (44 per cent) of unconvicted and a third (32 per cent) of convicted prisoners were unemployed prior to their imprisonment. These are shocking statistics and point to the importance of inequality in explaining crime.

Inequality

The two main forms of inequality are economic inequality and social inequality.

Economic inequality

Economic inequality is concerned with financial and material inequalities. It is not the same as poverty, for it is theoretically possible to have an unequal distribution of wealth, goods and services without having poverty. However, poverty can be described as the 'unacceptable face of inequality' (Alcock, 1993). Inequality and poverty also differ in the ways that it is thought they can be addressed. Alcock (1987), for example, notes how analyses of poverty tend to take place within Fabian or social democratic frameworks. This means it is thought that poverty can be tackled through the piecemeal intervention of the state. Alcock is right. If poverty could be defined, the state could, if it had the ideological and economic willingness to, tackle it. While the tackling of poverty is likely to have some effect upon extremes of inequality, it will not abolish inequality because, as more radical analysts (for example, Ginsburg, 1979; Gough, 1979; Novak, 1988) and the supporters of free markets (for example, Hayek, 1960; Friedman, 1962) tell us, material inequality is fundamental to capitalism, an issue we return to below.

Social inequality

Social inequalities refer to those inequalities that are the consequence of imbalances in power and status, for example inequalities of class, gender, 'race' and disablement. Economic and social inequalities are not mutually exclusive. So, for example, working-class people are more likely to have incomes towards the lower end of the income spectrum because of the structure of capitalist wage and labour markets. However, it is also the case that working-class men, on average, will have a higher income than working-class women. This is because in the case of women capitalism and patriarchy conjoin, meaning that women are exploited by capitalism in a different way to men because of their gender (for example, Massey, 1984; Beechey and Perkins, 1987).

Inequalities in contemporary society

We live in a deeply unequal society. The wealthiest 1 per cent of people in Britain own a quarter (23 per cent) of all the UK's marketable wealth. The wealthiest 50 per cent own the vast majority (95 per cent) of the UK's marketable wealth. This, of course, means that the poorest 50 per cent own only 5 per cent. Wealth is also concentrated among the very rich. So, for example, in 1976 the wealthiest 5 per cent owned over a third (38 per cent) of marketable wealth. By 2001 they owned 43 per cent (all figures are from National Statistics, 2003).

Marketable wealth is partly a reflection of income. Income inequality rapidly increased during the 1980s with the poorest quintile gaining an average of 0.4 per cent per year during the Thatcher years, compared to an annual average gain of 3.8 per cent for the richest quintile (Brewer et al., 2004). The Joseph Rowntree Foundation's *Inquiry into Income and Wealth* (Barclay, 1995) found that this dispersion was caused by an increase in the number of people reliant on state benefits, the level of which was not keeping pace with increases in average earnings, a stagnation of real wages for the lowest paid (men) and an increasingly regressive taxation regime. During the Major years (1990–96/7) inequality actually reduced as the income of the poorest quintile increased at a greater rate than the richest quintile (1.5 per cent compared to 0.5 per cent). Drawing upon Clark and Taylor (1999), Brewer et al. (2004: 13) argue that this was due to the recession of the early 1990s where the pattern of unemployment had a 'small equalising effect on the distribution of income'. Under New Labour (1996/7–2002/3) income inequality has stabilised, with the incomes of the richest and poorest quintiles rising, on average, at a similar rate of between 2 and 3 per cent per annum.

However, the Gini Coefficient – a measure showing the degree of inequality – demonstrates that there has been a statistically significant increase in inequality between 1996/7 and 2002/3. Brewer et al. (2004) argue that this increase has occurred because of what is happening to the income of the very richest and very poorest. Real incomes at the top end (beyond the 85th percentile) of the income distribution is growing more rapidly the higher the individual's income is. So, for example, the top 1 per cent have seen their income grow by over 4 per cent per annum between 1996/7 and 2002/3 due to increases in the remuneration of company executives and the cuts in the top rate of taxation that occurred in the 1980s. At the bottom end of the income distribution, income growth since 1996/7 is lower the poorer the individual is. For the poorest 2 per cent real incomes have actually fallen over the period 1996/7–2002/3. The reason for this is likely to be related to the non-take-up of social security benefits and because:

> ... total benefit income accruing to the bottom income decile group has barely risen in real terms over the period in question, averaging about 0.3 per cent a year. By contrast, benefit income growth in the second decile groups has been stronger, averaging over 2 per cent a year. (Brewer et al., 2004: 19)

What this means is that the substantial benefit changes and increases that New Labour have introduced have not benefited the very poorest (Piachaud and Sutherland, 2000).

As the most extreme face of inequality, poverty is notoriously difficult to define, but even on the government's own relative measure of those people living in households with an income below 60 per cent of the median, there were 12.5 million people (8.7 million adults and 3.8 million children) living in poverty in 2001/2 (Flaherty et al., 2004). This equates to about a fifth of the general population and a third of all children. Due to changes in labour and wage markets over half (52 per cent) of all children living in poverty were in households where there was at least one person in paid employment (Flaherty et al., 2004).

New Labour argues that it is committed to tackling child poverty, but has defined the measure of this in such a way that it is still unclear below what income a family can be considered to be poor (see Department of Work and Pensions, 2004). The way in which it has decided to tackle inequality through interventions at the poorer end of the income distribution is also problematic. The main way New Labour has prevented the poorest from becoming poorer has been to substantially increase benefits for the youngest children and to heavily subsidise the wages of low-paid workers employed for at least 16 hours a week. What this means is that employers are essentially being subsidised by the state for paying low wages. Because of this, employers have little incentive to pay wages far, if at all, above the National Minimum Wage (NMW), which itself has no automatic mechanism for annual increases. This means the NMW has the potential to become a maximum wage for a large proportion of the workforce rather than a minimum. There is every possibility that in future years the 'making work pay' strategy – the combination of subsidising low wages and the NMW (see Grover, 2005) – will itself help to reinforce inequalities through poverty-level wages.

As we have noted, there are often close connections between economic and social inequalities. This can be seen when we consider the gendered and racialised aspects of inequality. On average, women are more likely to have lower incomes compared to men. So, for example, they are more likely to live in poor households and, compared to men, a greater proportion appear in the bottom quintile of income groups (28 per cent of women compared to only 12 per cent of men) (Flaherty et al., 2004). This is because women are concentrated in low-paid and low-status employment, especially service sector employment, and the majority of lone parents are women. Lone mothers are particularly vulnerable to poverty. So, for example, over 50 per cent of lone mother households can be described as being poor compared to only 20 per cent of couple households with dependent children (Flaherty et al., 2004). Women's poverty is structured through patriarchy and capitalism, the consequence of which is an assumed dependency of women on men. This consequence of the alleged dependency of women upon men is the idea that women do not need to work at all or, if they do work, they can be paid less than men because they also have access to a (male) partner's wage.

People from minority ethnic groups are likely to have low incomes compared to majority ethnic people. So, for example, 18 per cent of white people are in the lowest quintile groups compared to a third (34 per cent) of black Caribbean people, 43 per cent of black non-Caribbean people and nearly two-thirds (61 per cent) of Pakistani and Bangladeshi people (Flaherty et al., 2004: 188). The poor financial and material conditions of many minority ethnic people are the result of racial discrimination. There are various arenas of discrimination. Discrimination in labour markets means both that the unemployment rate for minority ethnic people is higher than that for majority ethnic people and that black and minority ethnic people are concentrated in particularly low-paid sectors of the economy. In contrast, discrimination in the benefit system means that black and minority ethnic people have particular difficulties in accessing benefits they are entitled to (Gordon and Newnham, 1985; Walker and Ahmad, 1994). Discrimination in housing means that minority ethnic people are concentrated in the most deprived local authority districts and in social housing or in owner-occupation which is 'low quality, in undesirable inner-city areas, and owned by families without the resources to improve or maintain their home' (Flaherty et al., 2004: 197).

Crime and inequality

There is much evidence that points to important relationships between crime and inequality and the indicators of inequality, most notably unemployment. Box (1987: 87, original italics) reviewed the literature on crime and inequality and concluded that *'every study to date on income inequality and property offences or non-fatal violence shows there is a statistical, maybe even causal relationship'*. Box's conclusions were based mainly on North American studies. British studies are less numerous. However, they also point to a relationship between crime and inequality. Witt et al. (1998: 398), for example, concluded that 'high crime is associated with ... high wage inequality associated with the distribution of weekly earnings of full-time manual men'. Their focus was upon property crime and they also found high rates of such crimes were also associated with increases in male unemployment and high growth in the amount of thievable property. As an indicator of inequality it is the relationship between unemployment and crime that has been most intensely focused upon.

Between the mid-1970s and mid 1980s Chiricos (1987) argues that there was a 'consensus of doubt' about a positive relationship between unemployment and crime. However, since the mid-1980s the evidence suggests that there are positive relationships between various crimes and unemployment. So, for example, Elliott and Ellingworth (1998) found a significant and positive relationship between unemployment and property crime, while Hale (1998) and Carmichael and Ward (2000) found a similar relationship between unemployment and burglary, and Hale (1998) also between unemployment and robbery. Even a researcher from the Home Office (Field, 1990, 1999), while unable to find evidence of a general relationship between unemployment and crime, has found a potential causal relationship between unemployment and violence against the person.

All these studies are quantitative, comparing large sets of crime and unemployment data. The problem with this type of analysis is that it says little about whether it is unemployment that causes crime or crime that causes unemployment and, even if a correlation between unemployment and crime is found, whether it is unemployed people actually committing the crime (Farrington et al., 1986). To overcome such problems Farrington et al. interviewed individuals as part of the Cambridge Study in Delinquent Development (for example, Farrington, 1995; West and Farrington, 1973, 1977). Their interviews with young men suggested that crime rates were higher during periods of unemployment compared to periods of employment, particularly for crimes involving material gain.

Research by Stewart and Stewart (1993) also points to relationships between crime and inequality. They examined the material circumstances of nearly 1,400 young people who had mainly committed crimes of dishonesty. They found that two-thirds (64 per cent) of their respondents were unemployed. This was nearly ten times the unemployment rate for Great Britain which was 6.7 per cent at the time. They also found that 38 per cent of unemployed 17-year-olds in their study had no weekly income at all. Probation officers considered the poor financial situation of offenders and addiction to be the most important aspects of young people's social circumstances associated with their offending. In a related exercise Smith and Stewart (1997) compared the material circumstances of young probation clients in the early 1990s to that of probation clients in the mid-1960s. The material circumstances of probation clients had got markedly worse over the three decades. In 1991 only a fifth (21 per cent) of probation clients were employed compared to nearly 6 out of 10 (59 per cent) in 1965. The proportion of probation clients with no income at all was four times higher in 1991 compared to 1965.

Gender, crime and inequality

The available research suggests that there are close relationships between crime and inequality and its indicators of unemployment and poor material circumstance. However, much of it has focused upon males only. Naffine and Gale (1989) argue in the case of research on unemployment and crime that this is particularly problematic and reflects a sexism in the research which does not take seriously women's economic roles and which is confounded by researchers being 'less than forthcoming about the masculinity of their viewpoint' (p. 145). Naffine and Gale's research on relationships between female unemployment and crime in Australia found that: 'If criminologists were to commence their theorizing with female data, it is unlikely that they would draw a connection between unemployment and crime' (1989: 154).

Naffine and Gale's research is open to the Farrington et al. (1986) criticisms of macro-studies. What is more, if Farrington et al.'s guidance is pursued, it soon becomes clear that women's offending, if not structured through unemployment, is certainly structured through poverty. The best example of research examining the connections between poverty and female offending is that by Carlen (1988). Carlen found that the vast majority (34 of the 39 women she worked with) 'claimed that at least some of their crimes had been occasioned by either a necessity born of poverty or a perceived need born of consumerism' (Carlen, 1988: 113). Using a control theory framework Carlen argued that crime enabled the women in her study to resist their class and gender positions. In terms of class, crime allowed the women to secure items of necessity and to engage with the purchasing aspects of consumer culture without having to take 'crap jobs'. In terms of gender, crime allowed the women to resist patriarchy because it enabled them to separate from abusive men, either by supporting their own home or by using violence to tackle their oppressors.

In-depth interviews with males have shown some resonances with Carlen's work. So, for example, Willott and Griffin's (1999) focus was upon the ways in which a group of 66 working-class men who had committed 'money-related crimes' talked about their offending. They found that in contrast to the dominant discourses of criminality, their respondents constructed themselves as being 'Robin Hood'-type characters who, because of the state breaking its promises with regard to social provision (highlighted by rising unemployment, the dismemberment of the NHS and state-sponsored benefits), were:

> ... forced ... to 'become' criminal in order to continue as family breadwinners ... the men could represent themselves as morally sound and even heroic 'Robin Hood' figures – intent upon providing

for the basic needs of their families by the redistribution of wealth through activities that were legally classed as criminal. (Willott and Griffin, 1999: 457)

Over the past two decades the research evidence suggests that indicators of inequality such as (male) unemployment and poverty are closely related to crime. The relationship is probably not causal, for we know that middle-class people engage in criminal activity although they rarely get prosecuted, and we know that those social groups who endure poverty disproportionately are not necessarily the most criminogenic. So, for instance, while self-report evidence for young people demonstrates a similar rate of offending for females and males (Bowling et al., 1994), the accepted wisdom is that men commit more crime and, indeed, more serious crime than women, although, as we have seen, women are more concentrated in lower income groups. In the case of 'race' there is debate as to whether young black people are more likely to be involved in crime compared to their white counterparts (see Coleman and Moynihan, 1996), although the former are more disadvantaged in material terms.

Rather than seeking causal relationships, it is probably more useful, as critical criminologists argue, to think of crime having a number of 'determining contexts' (Chadwick and Scraton, 2001: 71). The evidence in this section has shown that one of those contexts is inequality. Given this evidence, the issue becomes why the connections between inequality and crime do not appear to be taken seriously by those charged with developing policies to address the 'crime problem'. It is to this issue that I now turn.

Personal responsibility and the disciplinarian state

On announcing New Labour's five-year crime strategy in July 2004 the Prime Minister, Tony Blair MP, argued that it marked the 'end of the 1960s liberal, social consensus on law and order' (Blair, 2004: 1). While this was an opening pitch for the 'law and order' vote for the 2005 general election, the comments of Blair were important because of the way he related the freedoms – of expression, lifestyle and the 'individual's right to live their own personal life in the way they choose' (Blair, 2004) – gained in the 1960s with the issue of responsibility. Referring to John Stuart Mill, Blair noted how freedoms always came with responsibility. Since the 1960s, however, crime policy was held to have got this balance out of kilter:

A society of different lifestyles spawned a group of young people who were brought up without parental discipline, without proper role models and without any sense of responsibility to or for others. (Blair, 2004: 2)

There was an ahistoric feel to Blair's speech. As the editorial in the *Guardian* (20 July 2004) noted, it was as if Blair had forgotten that

... [the] liberal consensus ended over a decade ago when a succession of hardline laws introduced by [then Conservative Home Secretary and now leader of the Conservative Party] Michael Howard were not only endorsed by Labour, but even implemented and extended by them from 1997.

Responsibility, the state and the Conservatives

The significance of the *Guardian*'s point lay in its highlighting of the continuity between the Conservative governments of the 1980s and the 1990s and New Labour. While they might like to claim as their own the importance of the idea of responsibility in crime and social policy, it has not been the preserve of New Labour. For the Conservatives the increasing crime rates of the 1980s and early 1990s reflected a social malaise that had its roots in a congruence of social and cultural change from the 1960s and an overly burdensome and invasive state. It was the moral authoritarianism and free market economics of the Conservatives that helped it to locate the social and economic problems Britain was facing as being an erosion of the protectors – patriarchy and capitalism – of harmony and stability. It was held that second-wave feminism was questioning the patriarchal order and working-class people were being encouraged by the trades unions to challenge the legitimacy of the capitalist order in disputes such as the miners' strikes (in 1972 and 1984/5), the Trico Folbreth strike (1976), the Imperial Typewriters strike (1976), the Grunwick Processing Laboratories strike (1976/7), the National Graphical Association action at the Grunwick works in Warrington (1983) and through the militancy of unions in state-owned enterprises such as British Leyland (see Dromey and Taylor, 1978; Callinicos and Simons, 1985; Thornett, 1998).

However, the structures of harmony and stability could only be challenged because the state allowed them to be so. Bloated with paternalism, the state was held to be protecting people from the inevitabilities of economic change, in particular the need to embrace global free markets, and encouraging, especially women, to make lifestyle choices (such as divorce and separation, and lone motherhood) that were held to be disastrous for social stability because of the ways in which they undermined the patriarchal order. To Thatcherite radicals, individuals had no reason to behave responsibly because they knew the state would buffer them from their own actions. It was in this context that work by right-wing American commentators, such as Charles Murray (1984, 1990, 1994) and Laurence Mead (1986), on relationships between state services and moral and economic well-being became influential. This work, in addition to impacting upon the thinking of the Right, was in the longer term to impact upon the thinking of the parliamentary Left.

For both Murray (1984, 1990, 1994) and Mead (1986) the problem with welfare benefits and services was that in contrast to tackling social problems, they were merely reproducing and concentrating them. This was because in various ways the state was usurping personal responsibility and discouraging social duty. Along with other authors (for example, Morgan, 1995) these studies supplied academic credence to the idea that what Britain required to address a perceived deep-rooted social malaise – most significantly demonstrated by increasing crime rates and dependency upon state benefits – was more restrictive access to state benefits and services. State intervention stood accused of encouraging irresponsibility, replacing what were once mutually organised support networks, including 'the family', and discouraging a sense of duty to others. For these writers it was not a surprise that Britain was facing increasing crime rates, social disorder and state dependency when the state seemed to be intent on destroying the protective factors of responsibility and duty.

The solution to these problems differed between authors. Murray saw individuals as being rational economic beings so the provision of welfare benefits merely acted as an incentive to irresponsibility. Hence, his solution to tackling dependency and its attendant problems was the withdrawal of welfare benefits. In contrast, Mead's explanation focused upon the character of the poor. He saw the long-term workless poor as being 'dutiful but defeated' and in need of 'help and hassle', reinforced by sanctions for those who do not co-operate (Deacon, 1997: xiv). For Mead, the issue was 'not the level of benefits but the terms and conditions on which they were paid' (Deacon, 2002: 50), meaning that benefits needed to be more authoritarian in character in order to clearly delineate the conduct required from individuals in return for those benefits.

Grover and Stewart (2002) have demonstrated the influence of these 'underclass'-type arguments upon Conservative governments of the 1980s and 1990s. However, Deacon (2000) argues that such arguments also had an impact upon the thinking of the Left, for the arguments of right-wing commentators meant that the Left could no longer ignore the issues of personal responsibility and social obligation in its own analyses of social problems. The engagement with responsibility and obligation came through two of the more enduring intellectual influences upon New Labour: ethical or Christian socialism and communitarianism, particularly that associated with moral philosopher Amitai Etzioni (1995, 1997).

Ethical socialism

Ethical socialism is important from our perspective because it 'is the doctrine of personal responsibility under virtually all social circumstances. People act under favourable and unfavourable conditions but remain responsible moral agents' (Halsey, 1993: x). In this context, inequality cannot condone offending behaviour because even the poorest have the opportunity to act in a law-abiding manner. Crime is something that individuals do, not because of their material circumstances, but because either they do not know how to act in a law-abiding way or they wilfully choose not to act in such a manner. Either way, they can and should be taught how to act responsibly without the state having to engage with the problem of their material circumstances. That education, as is discussed below, has come in the form of several draconian measures aimed at making sure parents in particular take their child-rearing responsibilities very seriously.

The starting point of Etzioni's brand of communitarianism is not that controversial, for he points out that the individualism upon which the unleashing of the free market was premised in the 1980s acted to undermine the sense of obligation to others. For Etzioni the unqualified individualism of the Right was not enough, as it had assumed, to secure social harmony. The effect was, in fact, the opposite: a tendency towards social disintegration. While Thatcherism in Britain and Reaganomics in the USA both stood for free markets and a moral authoritarianism that emphasised discipline and the importance of traditional institutions of socialisation, the two – because of the individualism of the former and the essentially social character of the latter – were contradictory. Abbott and Wallace (1992: 82) succinctly summarise the contradictions in their focus upon the politics of 'the family': 'the logical extension of economic liberalism is the fragmentation of the family, for why should a self-interested individual support a lot of dependants?'

It is Etzioni's analysis of the remedial actions required if a sense of obligation is to be fostered in contemporary society that is more controversial and the influence of his analysis can be seen in Blair's speech quoted at the beginning of this section. Etzioni believes that the individualism of Western societies has created an imbalance between the rights and responsibilities of individuals which means that there is more emphasis upon the 'rights of individuals, the enjoyment of which safeguards their freedom and enhances their personal autonomy' (Deacon, 2002: 64), than their responsibilities. This is problematic because in

Etzioni's analysis it is the acceptance of social responsibilities that 'maintains social order and enhances the communities in which they [individuals] live' (Deacon, 2002: 64). What is required in contemporary Western societies is a re-balancing of rights and responsibilities to emphasise the responsibilities one has to oneself, one's family and society more generally. By accepting these responsibilities the individual is accepting their social obligations to others, obligations that, if required, should be enforced by the 'community'. What this means is that 'communitarians share much of the judgementalism of Conservatives such as [Charles] Murray or [Laurence] Mead' (Deacon, 2002: 66).

Deacon (2002) describes the combination of Christian socialism and communitarianism as 'Anglicanised communitarianism', a form of communitarianism which privileges the idea of the duty-bound moral agent in New Labour's 'rights and responsibilities' agenda and which structures New Labour's approach to social problems. In this context any rights that are conferred upon individuals and/or their dependent children brings a set of responsibilities that must be fulfilled in order to access those rights. In this sense the provision of welfare benefits and services should 'seek to shape their [recipients] values and mould their characters' (Deacon, 2002: 76).

The emphasis on rights and responsibilities and attempts to change the behaviour of individuals can be seen in a number of policy developments that deal with so-called antisocial behaviour. These include parenting contracts for the parents of disruptive school children, parenting orders for those parents whose children break curfew and antisocial behaviour orders and the eviction of neighbours with challenging behaviour from social rented housing. All these developments assume that socially located processes, such as parenting and acting in a pro-social manner, are not affected by material circumstances. However, as Utting (1995: 2–3) notes, while '[l]iving on a low income in a run-down neighbourhood does not make it impossible to be an affectionate, authoritative parent … it undeniably makes it more difficult'. In the case of offending and antisocial behaviour the influence of Anglicanised communitarianism means that the material circumstances of such activities are ignored. Parents are condemned as being, at best, ineffective and, at worst, complicit in their children's behaviour (Goldson and Jamieson, 2002).

The observant reader may have spotted an inconsistency in the argument. If the disciplinary state is so concerned with individualising the causes of crime and antisocial behaviour why has it embarked upon social policy programmes, most notably the various New Deals for non-employed people, that are concerned *inter alia* with tackling crime and anti-social behaviour? The answer to this question lies in tensions created by communitarian thinking for, while it is noted that social justice requires a 'regime in which everyone's basic needs for life, health, liberty and hope are respected and addressed' (Selznick, 1998, cited in Deacon, 2002), we have seen that any state support in communitarian thought should be behaviour-contingent if responsibility is to be encouraged. This raises two issues. First, when conditionality for state-sponsored benefits and services is premised upon behaviour, the focus becomes the individual rather than the social conditions that structure their lives. The issue becomes poorer people rather than the problems that they face. This is particularly visible in the New Deal for Young People (NDYP).

New Deal for Young People

The premise of the NDYP is that there are enough jobs in the economy for young people to do. The demand side is argued to have been taken care of by New Labour's prudent economic management and supply-side measures, such as the introduction of the National Minimum Wage, are in place to provide the financial incentive to take paid employment. In such an economic regime why should there be any unemployed young people? The answer to this question is held to lie within the character of young unemployed people: they do not have the right attitude towards paid employment. Callinicos (2001: 62) summarises the argument:

> Assuming (as [Gordon] Brown [the Chancellor of the Exchequer] does) … if macro-economic stability is secured and the right supply-side measures are in place, any further unemployment is voluntary. Unemployment is in these circumstances a consequence of the dysfunctional behaviour of individuals who refuse to work, and this behaviour must in turn be caused either by their individual moral faults or by a more pervasive 'culture of poverty'.

Second, when the focus becomes the behaviour of the individual, then there has to be a way of disciplining the errant, for there is no guarantee that everyone will adhere to the responsibilities they are supposed to adopt. If this is the case, the state has to have some means of punishing the uncooperative. As we have noted, in communitarian thought responsibility is something that has to be enforced. The problem with this is that the punishment of irresponsibility can only be in those areas of life where the state has some degree of control. For poorer people these areas are their income and housing. Hence, poorer people are often forced to be responsible on the threat of having their benefit claims dismissed or having their benefit reduced. So, for example, the NDYP allows for the withdrawal of benefit from people deemed to be non-compliant for up to six months, that is potentially six months with no income at all. The evidence (Saunders et al., 2001) suggests that while the 26-week penalty is rarely used, 15 per cent of participants on the NDYP have had their benefit suspended for up to four weeks (Bivand, 2002). There are a number of issues raised by the use of such disciplinary mechanisms. First, the use of benefit suspensions merely helps to create inequality by deepening poverty. Therefore policies designed, at least in part, to tackle offending and which have been put forward in the criminological literature as a counter-effect to New Labour's free market thought (Downes and Morgan, 2002), can actually contribute to the social conditions that we have seen are conducive to offending.

Second, the disciplinary regime of programmes like the NDYP may encourage participants to disengage with the mechanism that is designed to integrate them into mainstream society. Young people have aired this concern with regard to the NDYP, noting that it 'will push some people into working in the illegal economy or into crime because they do not want to take any of the options'[1] (Bentley et al., 1999: 101). There is some empirical evidence that supports this line of thought, for a substantial minority of young people have disengaged with the NDYP. To September 2002 a third (29 per cent) of young people left the new deal for unknown reasons. The government argues that many of these will have left for paid employment, but the evidence that this is the case is not convincing (Hales and Collins, 1999). The problem is that while we know that some 173,000 (1 in 10) of 16–18-year-olds are not in paid employment, education or training (Social Exclusion Unit, 2000), it is unclear how many 18–24-year-olds are not.

Similar contradictions have been introduced by the trend towards reducing or withdrawing social security benefits to punish offenders for their wrong-doing. The Child Support, Pensions and Social Security Act 2000 allows Income Support and means-tested Jobseekers' Allowance to be reduced or withdrawn from individuals who break the conditions of their community orders. Results from the pilot scheme of the withdrawal of benefit scheme make the point: 'For some offenders, the main way they reported supporting themselves during the sanction period was through offending' (Knight et al., 2003: 57). As one respondent told Knight et al. (2003: 58): 'I just thought "f*** [sic] it, I'm going back to burgling". I'd stopped, I hadn't done one for ages.' It is likely that respondents were offending in order to survive, for they reported having 'problems paying for food, heating and electricity' (Knight et al., 2003: 58) because of their reduced benefit levels.

Conclusion

This chapter has demonstrated that there are close connections between inequality and crime. It would be fair to say that these connections are understood in government. We have seen that there have been social policy developments that, for example, link the unemployment of young people with crime. However, a concern with personal responsibility and social obligation, structured through Anglicanised communitarianism, means that those social policies which could offset the worst excesses of inequality are often behaviour-contingent. The consequence of this is that unless poorer people are held to be acting in a responsible manner, they are in danger of being forced further into poverty.

If one of the driving factors of criminology is the delineation of the criminal from the law-abiding, then the criminologist must engage with such issues. Criminology needs to be as much about social policy and social justice as it is about criminal justice. On the one hand, this is not a unique observation. After all, inequality has had a central explanatory role in sociological approaches to crime since at least the work of Robert Merton (1938) on anomie and strain (see Chapter 1). On the other hand, this needs to be reiterated because criminology rarely engages with the detail of social policy. However, given that it is through social policy interventions at the lower end of income distribution that the state attempts to tackle the worst excesses of inequality, then criminology must engage with such issues because, as we have seen, the operation of social policies can have the effect of making poor people even poorer. This is a shorter-term project for criminology.

The longer-term project must be to recapture the arguments of 1970s radical criminology (for example, Taylor et al., 1973) which aimed to 'promote a form of radical politics' (Muncie, 2001: 187). While radical criminology has been widely criticised, its basic premise that the relations of production and ownership shape the interventions of the state, whether in relation to crime or social policy still holds. For example, the social policy developments highlighted in this chapter have been discussed in the context of the contemporary socio-political concerns with personal responsibility, but capitalist imperatives also structure those concerns. The new deals, for example, are held by New Labour to have a role in the managing of crime and disorder, but they also act to supply labour to capital as cheaply as possible (see Grover and Stewart, 2002). It is here that analyses of crime and social policy have common ground, for while the inequalities of patriarchal capitalism provide the context for much offending behaviour, they are also reproduced through social policy interventions that are designed to meet the longer-term needs of capital.

Note

1   The 'options' stage of the NDYP is a six-month period in which conscripts are expected to take part in one of four possible schemes: paid employment which is subsidised by the state, education, a placement with a voluntary organisation or a place with the environmental taskforce.

Chapter 5

Burning issues: fire, carnival and crime

Mike Presdee

Introduction

On Monday, 6 December 2004 in Indian Head, Washington, USA, unknown arsonists put a complete new upmarket housing development to the 'torch', burning 26 houses in one spectacular conflagration! It was a five million pound bonfire that was deliberate and organised, changing both the landscape and society in one swift and totally destructive act (*Independent on Sunday*, 13 December 2004). But what was its meaning?

Here I want to explore in a cultural criminological sense the 'story' of fire, the state's fear and criminalisation of fire and the fascination of fire within everyday life. Fire is always about context, and specifically social context, being not just a 'technology' but also an interaction with social events and relationships. There is a tension between fire and society that is human and it is this human context that I wish to explore here. It involves the rational/scientific use of purification by fire, such as the deoderisation of 'smell'; the cooking of putrefied meat; and the forging of metals in the purifying of rock. But it also involves human emotions entangled with fire. Fire is indeed 'useful' and its uses have been socially organised but it is also pleasurable in many ways, making fire more a social reality rather than a natural reality. As Bachelard poetically points out: 'Fire smoulders in a soul more than it does under the ashes. The arsonist is the most dissembling of criminals' (Bachelard 1964: 13).

Through the quest for pleasure we all have the potential to become dissembling deceivers. In a more consumer-driven society do we become less receptive to pleasure? Do we have less pleasure? Do we as a result seek more than ever before the pleasure hidden within transgression? The pleasure of fire!

However, there is another dimension. Why is it that 'fire' attracts, creates, destroys? Why is it so central to all our lives – possessed, controlled, criminalised? Where does its power come from? Bachelard, in his *Psychoanalysis of Fire*, observed in his typical philosophical and poetic way that:

> Fire and heat provide modes of explanation in the most varied domains, because they have been for us the occasion for un-forgettable memories, for simple and decisive personal experiences. Fire is thus a privileged phenomenon which can explain anything. If all that changes slowly may be explained by life, all that changes quickly is explained by fire. Fire is the ultra-living element. It is intimate and it is universal. It lives in our heart. It lives in the sky. It rises from the depths of the substance and offers itself with the warmth of love. Or it can go back down into the substance and hide there, latent and pent up, like hate and vengeance. Among all phenomena, it is really the only one to which there can be so definitely attributed the opposing values of good and evil. It shines in Paradise. It burns in Hell. It is gentleness and torture. It is cookery and it is apocalypse. It is well being and it is respect. It is a tutelary and a terrible divinity, both good and bad. It can contradict itself; thus it is one of the principles of universal explanation. (Bachelard, 1964: 7)

Background

In any one week in England and Wales there are on average 2,100 deliberately set primary fires recorded that result in at least 2 deaths, 55 injuries and a cost of £40 million. Here a 'primary' fire is officially defined as 'Any recorded fire incident that occurs in buildings or property, or where there are any casualties or where 5 or more appliances attend' (Office of the Deputy Prime Minister, 2004a: 3). The bulk of these fires involve the burning of cars with approximately 200 burnt out every day, while 17 schools and 4 churches or places of worship suffer an arson attack every week and in the last decade there have been 2.4 million recorded arson fires, 32,000 injuries and 1,200 deaths (Office of the Deputy Prime Minister, 2004b). Recorded offences continue to rise massively. In 1963 there were only 1,129 recorded offences which by 2002/3 had exploded to 53,200 with 103,000 deliberate fires reported to the fire and rescue service.

Yet detection rates remain low at only 8 per cent compared to 24 per cent for all other offences. This low detection rate results in low conviction rates. For example, there were only 450 convictions in 1963 that rose only to 2,000 in 2003 (Office of the Deputy Prime Minister, 2003). Of those found guilty at Magistrates' Court, 60 per cent were under 18 years of age and 32 per cent under 15 years. Of those found guilty at a Crown Court, only 32 per cent were under 21 years of age (Office of the Deputy Prime Minister, 2004c).

This can be contrasted to the USA where in 2002 there were 44,500 intentionally set 'structure' fires reported, plus 41,000 deliberately set vehicle fires, resulting in 350 civilian deaths at a cost of $1.2 billion. When outdoor fires and a proportion of suspicious fires are added, this rises to an annual cost of $2 billion (US Fire Administration, 23 June 2004). Overall 52 per cent of arson arrestees are under 18 years, while only 2 per cent of fire setters are convicted (National Fire Protection Association, 2000).

As always, official statistics only include recorded and reported incidents. But the intrinsic nature of fire and its place and meaning within the social and cultural activities of everyday life make it impossible to even begin to attempt to estimate the actual numbers of deliberate fires, big and small, that happen in any one day. At specific times of the year, such as the weeks leading up to and preceding the fire festivals of Halloween and Guy Fawkes night, we experience a festival of fire where 'fire and fireworks [are] celebrated throughout Britain, [which] literally lights up the country in a veritable carnival of noise and destruction that excites all classes and all ages' (Presdee, 2000: 31). Destruction through fire becomes at this time a central cultural activity for the great majority of the country. This is a time when arson is both practised and celebrated by millions.

What is surprising is that there has been no real cultural analysis within criminology of the causes or genesis of arson with studies, instead, concentrating on the small number of offenders convicted (Soothill and Pope, 1973; Soothill et al., 2004a). A more cultural criminological approach can excavate the place and meaning of fire in a social and historical sense, bringing a greater depth and understanding to the question as to why at this time we are experiencing an increasing fascination with fire that results in both death and destruction. As I have remarked elsewhere:

> ... cultural criminology reflects ... the history of the discourses of 'limit' and 'transgression'; 'boundary making' and 'boundary breaking'; 'control' and 'hedonism'; 'rationality' and 'irrationality', alongside the examination of the 'inner' experience of individuals

free from moral reasoning and safe from the 'outside' world. The individual 'inner' experience becomes the seat of wrongdoing and immorality par excellence. It is when this inner experience becomes exteriorized into the rebelliousness and resistance of carnival (or fête) that disorder becomes defined as law breaking rather than harmless fun – much the same way in which there is an instance when the fascination with fire becomes arson. (Presdee 2004: 278)

Experience is, then, the end product of the needs and dilemmas that we all face in everyday life, being no more or less than social action reified. There are only rare times when social action is truly 'senseless', therefore we need to explore not events or incidents but the social context within which such incidents occur. As Ferrell (2005) suggests 'experiences and emotions have also come into focus as part of cultural criminology's emphasis on everyday existence as an essential arena of criminality and control. Cultural criminology highlights the currents of carnivalesque excitement, pleasure, and risk-taking that animate everyday life, but equally so the many capillaries of daily control designed to contain and commodify these experiential currents.'

Cultural criminology attempts to articulate deeper and wider 'human concerns', 'expectations' and 'yearnings' than methods of enquiry that are bound by the methodological constraints and shackles of ascertainable evidence, rather than a more creative criminology that attempts 'to reflect the peculiarities and particularities of the late-modern socio-cultural milieu' (Hayward, 2004a: 155–63).

Within this theoretical context I want now to explore the ways in which fire has become an important part of the culture of everyday life and is more and more becoming an integral act of rebelliousness and resistance, defiance and destruction. Throughout I have used writings on fire produced for me by final-year students at one 'high school' in the South East of England, who wrote about their experiences as well as their feelings for fire and what it meant to them. The original spelling has been retained in the extracts presented, as well as fictional names of both schools and pupils. Also I have returned to 'field notes' that I made while observing the actions of a group of young people in the Longlevens district of Gloucester on 'bonfire' night of 1999.

The meaning of fire

The element we call fire has been a central phenomenon in the development of both the natural and human worlds and has been a part of the process of shaping terrains, the countryside, flora and fauna, and also human societies and their ways of living. Since early primitive societies, humankind has remained frightened yet fascinated by fire with its innate and immense power to destroy and create. Early humans quickly learned that it gave both light and warmth and that it might keep predators at bay through its central overwhelming ability to frighten.

Humans quickly learned to cook their prey and, as they watched natural fire chase animals from forests, they began to use the power of fire to kill and destroy as their prey were driven over cliffs, into clearings or marshes where hunters waited for the kill (Barnouw, 1979; Goudsblom, 1992; Pyne, 1995). They also noticed the abundance of new growth that happened after fires and began a crude and simple form of farming with fire. In other words, they began to play with the awesome power of fire, its destructive ability on the one hand and its creativeness on the other. The fascination with fire had led to playing with fire.

For Freud the beginning of civilisation only begins with this ability to retain and control fire when he suggested in a footnote in *Civilisation and its Discontents* that:

> ... primal man had the habit, when he came in contact with fire, of satisfying an infantile desire connected with it, by putting it out with a stream of urine ... The first person to renounce this desire and spare the fire was able to carry it off with him and subdue it to his own use. (Freud, 1955)

Lévi-Strauss (1975) also saw the importance of the mastery of fire for human culture and development when he concluded that culture and creativity were not possible until humankind moved from eating the uncooked to the cooked, thereby beginning the social and cultural ritualisation of eating and social interplay.

The importance of fire to the continuance of social life led inevitably to fire becoming an important aspect of social and cultural life wherever and whenever societies developed and quickly found its way into the ceremonies and celebrations of social life. Fire marked both life and death, the beginning and end of seasons, the powerful and the powerless. Whoever had the technology to create fire at random became the alchemists of ancient societies holding as they did the power to change minerals into either weapons or tools. Here was the power to destroy or create held within one magical ability, to make fire for whoever, whenever, wherever. They became the professional players with fire and in the absence of any notion of science became the 'keepers' of life, the wardens of the passage through life to death and therefore the early priests of primitive religions and spirituality.

This duality of destructiveness and creativity, held within the abstraction of fire, resulted in a profound polarity buried deep within the consciousness of human cultures to the extent that it seems now in contemporary society to be a natural and therefore instinctive, innate and emotional cultural response to fire. But it is in reality the result of social actions over time, played out through social structures and relationships that have slowly manifested themselves through forms and formations of culture. Fire has slowly permeated our emotional makeup entering our cultural consciousness in a deep and layered way. Fear yet fascination; destruction yet creation; death yet life – these dualities of fire lie buried within us, erupting from time to time, whenever and wherever the passage or survival of social life and social identity becomes a burning issue.

> At the Bay High when year 11 leaves they get their ties, tie them round lamp-posts and set them alight for leaving and surviving school. It's a celebration thing. (Ellie, 17)

> Last year on the last day at school before the summer holidays all the year 12s was burning their blazers!! There were fires all down the road! You couldn't wear those again!! (Jackie, 17)

For these young people the power of fire was used to mark their passage from one social era to another. To destroy the power of adults and in so doing create a new future they hoped would be theirs.

The possession of fire enabled humans to literally play at god, to control life, to conquer and create yet also to resist, thus moulding our emotional responses to the possibility of its power. Ancient tyrants could install fear through the burning of towns and villages yet the oppressed could, in turn, use fire to destroy the possessions of the tyrant, making fire a genuine tool of resistance. The same fear and the same resistance can be achieved through the burning of a car in contemporary Canterbury – the same fears, the same fascinations and the same feeling of power.

Fête and fire

My field notes of a trip to a housing estate in Gloucester on November 5th, Bonfire Night, tells the story of a large group of young men and young women who lit a fire in a quiet place on their estate, away from the official adult-controlled displays. I positioned myself on the far side of the field in which they gathered and watched as they performed their own spectacle of fire. My notes went on to describe the 'spectacle' as follows:

The young people danced in the fire, bouncing on mattresses placed over the fire. Like Fijian fire walkers they danced and dared each other to stay in the fire longer and longer. They dangled ropes into the heat of the flames and hurled them out and swung the burning ends around their heads. Later they withdrew to the black corner of the green and watched the dying fire and sat listening to the background staccato bursts of shell fire.

Then they got wooden boards and placed those over the fire and as the flames rekindled the fire dance began again. They faced each other bouncing on the bridges of burning boards, jousting with each other with burning sticks as the howling wind made the flames more dangerous. Like mediaeval knights they fought in the fire and the watching crowd feasted on this spectacle of fire.

Then they noticed me sitting in the darkness of the trees and began to advance swinging the burning ropes above their heads. They began to charge and, as they got closer, I saw both young men and young women laughing, excited by this unexpected chase. As the fire sticks and ropes got closer I left them to their spectacle and to their fire.

This celebration of fire through fire festivals is a cultural acceptance of its power and its properties. Halloween, a Christian festival tacked onto the Celtic pagan fire festival of Samhain, celebrated the autumn solstice and the move from light to darkness and the importance of fire for life. Bakhtin talked of the Roman fire festival of 'Moccoli' and its importance in everyday life.

> The heart of the matter is the ambivalent combinations of abuse and praise, of the wish for death and the wish for life, projected in the atmosphere of the festival of fire, that is of burning and re-birth ... (Bakhtin, 1984: 248)

Bakhtin also described renaissance fire festivals such as the one Rabelais attended in Rome in 1549 which was 'performed in a piazza, a battle was fought with dramatic effects, fireworks, and even casualties ... The traditional hell was presented in the form of a globe ejecting flames' (Bakhtin, 1984: 158).

Modern festivals continued to be popular on a global level. In Europe midsummer fires were described by Sir James Frazer in *The Golden Bough* as having 'three great features ... bonfires, the procession with torches round fields and the custom of rolling a wheel' (1922). There was much throwing of fire and jumping through flames as, like Prometheus playing with fire stolen from the gods, the meaning of fire became lost in folklore while the excitement, the fear and the fascination remained.

This fascination with danger and excitement was a continual theme within the writing of my group of young people:

> I think people like fire because its dangerous. The danger of fire encourages excitement. Every year I go to the bonfire and everyone really enjoys themselves. I think its because its fascinating for people to see something nice like a table turn into ash in seconds. Fires are a bit unpredictable which creates suspense for people. (Becky, 17)

> Fire … looks nice it looks soft and elegant. Its interesting and strange and it can destroy so much. I remember once when 4 or 5 best friends come round and we were sitting in the garden not doing very much and then my cousin got a lighter and some tissue and burnt it in front of us. It was fascinating because it flowed through the tissue, curling it and turning it into nothing. It looked so beautiful but it has an immense power to destroy everything. (Melissa, 17)

> I have a fascination for burning candles. Especially big ones and watch them disintegrate. They melt into all sorts of grotesque shapes. I just watch the flame go right down to the bottom…then there's nothing. (Hannah, 17)

In America the 'burning man' festival attracts 30,000 people to a celebration of creativity and then destruction, as people of all ages descend on the Black Rock Desert of Nevada to transgress through an orgasm of pyro-fetishism. In Japan, the Nachi, Kurama and Oniyo fire festivals are the biggest, while the Dosojin fire festival involves much fighting with and throwing of fire like the Samoan Fire Knife dancing annual championships that celebrate fighting with fire.

It is through these official carnivals that 'misrule', 'resentment' and 'resistance' are lived out as the 'logic of late capitalism' asserts itself within the weave of everyday life. It is at this moment that the need for the carnivalesque, the search for the carnivalesque, becomes an essential element within the culture of everyday lived life as we seek to find solace in transgression in order to free ourselves from the rules, regulations and regimentation of rational contemporary life. In some way the carnivalesque promises freedom.

Carnival, excitement and fire in everyday life

In contemporary everyday life the fascination with fire continues within a society where identity is forged through a process of consumption that demands an extreme individualism marked by hedonism and uncertainty. Bakhtin in his discussion of the need for carnival saw that 'capitalism created the conditions for a special type of inescapable solitary consciousness' (1984: 287–8), a solitariness caused, according to Weber, by 'puritan … ascetism turned against one thing: the spontaneous enjoyment of life and all it had to offer' (1984: 167–8). This spontaneity is where the formation of identity is forged. Without it we feel strait-jacketed and shoe-horned into a constricted and restricted way of life where consumption is central and where to 'have' is to exist and where to 'have nothing' is to be 'nothing'. The creation of 'things', consumer items, becomes ruled by rational processes as the conveyer belt of production becomes the only rational way of life as late-modernity becomes characterised by life determined by the collective experience of the stifling nature of 'rational production' on the one hand, and the individual loneliness of consumption on the other. There can be no place for emotions within the productive process while the process of consumption depends on it.

It is in the activities of everyday life that we come to negotiate and manoeuvre our way through the imperatives of production and consumption. Here in everyday life is where we create the 'impulse that drives us to unsettle or confound the fixed order of things', as 'our shifting sense of ourselves as subjects and as objects, as acting upon and being acted upon by the world, of being with and without certainty, of belonging and being estranged.' These combine to produce a contemporary culture of loneliness and loss of certainty (Jackson, 1989: 2). We struggle to assert ourselves, demanding to be taken notice of, to say we exist, as we strive to be considered free agents in a world of enforced rationalism. Banging on the boundaries created by rationalism is how we can express our humanity as we make our existence real through real social action. Empty lives become filled through transgressing the boundaries set for us. The performance of transgression makes up for the lack of spontaneity in contemporary everyday life as we transport ourselves from the realm of the mundane to the world of excitement. This 'lust for life' is what I think Weber meant by 'eudaemonism' or what Nietzsche called 'Dionysianism'. An 'unending turbulent lust and longing … that drives (us) to conquest, to drunkenness, to mystic ecstasy (through drugs), to love-deaths … and cannot be long restrained.' (Brinton, 1941: 39).

If you get a bottle and fill it with, like, body spray stuff and put it on the floor, light it and jump on it, the flame shoots out the end! Its really, really, exciting!! (Jessica, 17)

The thing about fires which personally pleases me, is the excitement of getting caught! Knowing that I would be in trouble if I was caught lighting a big fire with my friends … it excites me. (Megan, 17)

This cultural process presents to us the possibility of reconciliation with real life and through it, the setting fire to a car, or indeed fighting a fire as a 'fire fighter', can make us feel human and is proof that we 'exist'. Fire is a very conspicuous spectacle, as is television and film. It is seen by many, enjoyed by many and like conspicuous consumption, conspicuous spectacle has become an integral part of the process of identity formation. If we are what we consume, then we come alive through the spectacle we create! As Bakhtin remarked, 'The most intense and productive life of culture takes place on the boundaries' (1984: 191).

However, the breaking of boundaries and the urge to resist rules and regimentation in the past often found expression within the spectacle of carnival. Here was a world turned inside out as well as 'upside down' where, in the case of fire, its characteristics could be explored, celebrated and practised. Yet in contemporary society the licence for misrule is no longer held by the structure and constraints of carnival and so determined by those who took part, but is now held by the state and exercised through law and legislation. In other words, licensed misrule becomes captured and contained within the rational processes that make up the modern bureaucratic state. For late-modernity, carnival is dead but the need to transgress and resist is not and, although it is 'increasingly difficult to take to the streets or indeed to party' (Presdee, 2000: 45), carnival life, transgressive life, still happens in the creases of everyday life, creating instability, disorder and disturbance. 'It is as if, through the dual forms of scientific rationality and containment, carnival has shattered and its fragments and debris are now to be found in a wide variety of contemporary forms, but hardly ever, ironically, in the remaining shell of what is still called carnival' (Presdee, 2000: 45).

The fire of carnival that I mentioned earlier now becomes part of the 'debris' of carnival driven into the back alleys of cities where fires erupt in a seemingly spontaneous fashion as cars, fences, rubbish bins and back-yard doors disappear, consumed in the flames of transgressive burning transformed into spectacles of the sublime. Through such acts we become once more acquainted with our lost or hidden humanity, underlining our need for relationships rather than politics. The memories of a lost life can literally be burnt away, cleansing the feelings of humiliation created by the confusions arising from the loss of identity.

> If you've had a bad day and you light a fire and burn something, its as if you are burning that bad day away. I know of a lot of people who have had bad experiences in their lives and feel that by burning a fire they are burning that bad experience. (Megan, 17)

> Fire can also get rid of memories, you can set light to the past and move on. (Tom 17)

The search for the sublime

This search for the sublime that I have just described has long been recognised as a motivational force that has become heightened under the imperatives of late capitalism. In the discourse of transgression it is associated with the 'edge work' described by Lyng and others (2004) that gives us the sublime experience of transgression. As I have suggested in the past:

> There can be no more exciting way of doing 'edge-work' for the 'law-abiding' than 'law-breaking'. Transgressing takes us to the very edge of 'lawfulness', where we stand and stare into the canyon of 'lawlessness'. It takes us to the edge of all that is approved of and defined as respectable. It carries the threat of being sent into social oblivion tantalizingly held before us, with its accompanying promise of a life as an outsider, to be dominated by the degradation of the rejected. We are confronted by the challenge of being lawless every day as we gamble, play with and push to the limits the fine line between order and disorder. The more successful the gamble becomes, the more heightened becomes the associated pleasure. (Presdee, 2000)

This 'heightened pleasure' becomes transformed into a 'sublime' experience that springs from the font of danger and excitement but, unlike extreme sports, this is a subliminal experience that emanates from the possibility of social death rather than physical mortality. Crime and, therefore, arson is social edgework where there is a risk of a social fall rather than a physical fall. It is, put simply, the blending together of pleasure and terror through transgression. Coleridge called it a 'delightful terror' and a 'fantastic pleasure' and John Ruskin, in a letter to his father from Chamonix in 1863, talked of the need for fear and danger which he felt made a 'better man, fitter for every sort of work and trial and nothing but danger produces this effect' (Macfarlane, 2003: 85). In 1688 John Dennis, when in the Alps, talked of walking on 'the very brink of destruction ... the sense of all this produced different emotions in me viz a delightful horror, a terrible joy, and at the same time that I was infinitely pleased, I trembled' (Macfarlane 2003: 72).

There is, then, a feeling of the sublime to be salvaged from the socially destructive nature of crime and arson. Fire is in itself a source of fear and terror which is heightened by the edgework involved in breaking the law, making arson the 'sublime' crime par excellence. As Edmund Burke pointed out in his *Philosophical Enquiry into the Origin of our Ideas of the Sublime and Beautiful* (1757 and 1990) 'any sort of terror ... is a source of the sublime, that is, it is productive of the strangest emotion which the mind is capable of feeling.'

> A couple of years ago my friends and I got an old wheely bin that had been in this field, filled it with leaves and branches and set fire to it. It was well fun. We knocked it over and then my friend started to run through it. I waited for my turn and felt sick. I didn't want to show I was frightened. Just before my turn it got bigger and started to spread so we all jumped through it. The flames seemed huge. It was brilliant and my shoes started to melt. (Vicky, 17)

Performance and everyday life

One of the characteristics of contemporary everyday life is the way that the media has blurred the delineation between drama and reality as both TV and film seek to present the spectacle of 'drama' and 'performance' to a mass audience. If we consider that the term 'drama' is Greek for action, then we can come to understand how action can be misunderstood as drama. The structures of drama, theatre, performance create certain limits on action, certain disciplines that restrict the social outcome. But experimental drama attempts to break through, to fracture theatre, in an attempt to get close to the 'real', get close to the energy of the real, until performance becomes real and the real becomes performance. Now the performative dimension of everyday life produces fire as theatre without vicarious experience. In other words, if you cannot 'play with' life (the vicarious) then you do 'reality'. Cars or buildings for burning become reified objects separated out from reality and ripe for ritualistic destruction; they become the props of spectacle and performance. If you cannot make drama, you make reality through the performance of transgression and it is through playing, through performance that we come to 'realise' what we want to be. If we play tough, we become the representation of toughness thereby redefining the 'self' through performance. From being dull to being interesting. From being powerless to being powerful. From being a nobody to a somebody. From meaningless to meaningful. Culture brings power, no matter the form of culture, be it the drama of theatre or drama of the street. For young people, fire culture, fire theatre, is permeated with power which spectators are powerless to stop in the same way as an audience cannot stop a murder in a play. Once the performance of fire begins, then there is an inevitability held within the dramatic dynamics of reality. A fire happens or is caused to happen:

> A crowd gathers to see what's going on. The crowd makes a circle around the event ... Talk in the crowd is about what happened, to whom, why ... Even after the event is 'cleaned up' some writing marks the site. For example, bloodstains, knots of witnesses, and the curious. Only slowly does the event evaporate and the crowd disperse. I call such events eruptions. (Schechner, 1988: 159)

In lives with no history and no future then the immediate is where we forge our identities. We perform, we present ourselves literally in the present. Nothing else is important, not consequences, not tomorrow, only the performance of now.

In the background of everyday life we can hear the shrill shouts of the political classes protesting against the social activities of the dispossessed as they make clumsy attempts to control social behaviour through absurd 'antisocial behaviour' legislation. At the same time, politicians create paternalistic and protective social policies supported by an army of social workers who set out to salve the collective guilt of the 'chattering' classes. The more politicians attempt forgiveness for their failure to achieve real change through social policy the more extreme will be the actions of those who seek more meaning in their lives than being the thankful poor. As I have stated elsewhere:

> ... we are all acutely aware that nothing has really started (politically) simply because nothing has really come to an end (inequality). The political promises of progress, equality and liberty are woven into the seams of history alongside the threads of failure. (Presdee, 2004b: 42)

It is in the social relationships of everyday life that we learn of the 'unpleasant social facts' that we are continually confronted with as we grow older: that we will never be affluent, never be fully educated/ schooled, never be equal. Parents and politicians conspire to protect the young as slowly horizons narrow rather than widen as the realities of a powerless life, indeed dare we say a working-class life, begin to be realized (Presdee, 2004b: 45). This is the great trick of modernity, full of the mischievous lies of life, where we learn that the world as we will live it is far from the social world that we desire or want.

Conclusion

In the end the festival of fire, the sublime experience of fire, the spectacle of fire, the performance of fire, provides an element to everyday life that means more than all the failed rational social policies of the past or on offer for the future. To understand why 'fire' has become such a 'burning issue' at this particular moment then politicians, policy-makers and crimi- nologists need to understand the everyday experience of a life lived within the constraints and constrictions of policies created by one group to make rational another, in other words, policies that make, for politicians, an ordered world – neat, tidy but unbearable to those who live within it. Fire is a response to the unbearable nothingness of contemporary life and brings fun, meaning and resistance to the meaninglessness of the political, rational world inhabited by both politicians and policy-makers alike.

Chapter 6

Drug and alcohol studies: key debates in the field

Fiona Measham

Introduction

The field of drug and alcohol studies is a rapidly expanding one, both as a subject area in its own right and also as an increasingly significant part of undergraduate and postgraduate criminology courses in the UK. This chapter introduces some key aspects of the field of drugs and alcohol,[1] attempting to show the fascination and passion of the subject and the ways in which the field provides an excellent illustration of key challenges and debates within the broader discipline of criminology. The chapter will consider: the way that a study of drugs demands a multidisciplinary approach; the significance of defining and measuring illicit drug use; the importance of historical, social and cultural context to an understanding of the subject area; and the relationship between drugs, crime and crime causation.

Policy issues surrounding enforcement and treatment are explored alongside the relationship between commercial development and control, using 'the world's favourite drug' – alcohol – as an example (Edwards, 2000). Through issues such as these, the chapter will provide not only an introduction to key debates within the field of drugs but I will also argue that changes in the last twenty years in terms of not only patterns of use but also theoretical and policy developments have significantly and irrevocably changed this subject area, both as an emergent sub-discipline of criminology and a distinct field served by a growing academic and professional base.

To understand drugs demands a multidisciplinary approach, meaning that good quality theoretical, empirical and policy-oriented research in the subject is currently informed by developments in a range of disciplines which includes sociology, social policy, history, psychology, health studies, gender studies, cultural studies, biology, anthropology, geography and chemistry. While individual studies may lean towards or be rooted in one particular discipline, a complete understanding of the research question is not possible without an awareness, for example, of historical, criminological, medical and sociological developments of relevance to the subject area. For example, it has been suggested that the principal British legislation surrounding the prohibition of psychoactive drugs – the 1971 Misuse of Drugs Act – is in need of substantial reform because it is rooted in an outdated and overridingly medical model of illicit drug use, whose core framework contains a medico-legal classification which grades severity of misdemeanour according to levels of known harm from individual drugs controlled by the Act (Shiner, 2003). However, while there has been a move towards multidisciplinary and indeed multi-method research design in the social sciences and particularly in drug research, this is not without its own challenges (e.g. Curtis, 2002; Singer, 2003).

Sources of knowledge

As with the study of other criminal behaviours, how we define and measure illicit drug use exercises much contemporary drug research. The significance of the broader criminological debate about sources of knowledge such as official statistics, self-report studies and victimisation surveys is effectively illustrated when asking even an apparently straightforward question such as how many people are engaged in the consumption or supply of illicit drugs in the UK. While regular Home Office bulletins provide the official statistics on the numbers of drug-related offenders and offences (e.g. Ahmad and Mwenda, 2004), these figures are clearly affected by criminal justice policy and practice.

The British Crime Survey is an important supplement to these official statistics and illustrates the enormous gulf between known drug offenders and the 'dark figure' of drug offences occurring in the UK, as discussed in standard criminology textbooks (e.g. Coleman and Moynihan, 1996). Given that the British Crime Survey is the only annual, national, representative household survey of the prevalence of drug use in the country, it provides invaluable and robust data on national and regional trends in drug use. Certainly it could be argued that the British Crime Survey provides a conservative estimate of prevalence of drug use due to, firstly, the response rate (74 per cent in 2002/3) and, secondly, the research design of private household surveys such as these which by definition exclude the homeless and those living in prisons, hospitals, hostels and other institutions. Those not living in private households or not at home when British Crime Survey interviewers call might be more likely to have higher levels of experience of crime, both as victims and as offenders, including drug offences (Condon and Smith, 2003). However, the British Crime Survey is only a starting point. Beyond these government-funded surveys, a lively drug research community exists in the UK and elsewhere which produces a wide range of empirical studies not only on the prevalence of illicit drug use, but also exploring the meanings, motivations, circumstances and consequences of illicit drug use and supply, alongside theoretical and policy discussions.

Disproportionality: the example of cannabis

While the critique of criminological sources of information such as official statistics, household victimisation surveys and self-report studies is a well covered criminological debate, it is by no means stale or conclusive because it sheds light not only on drug offences per se but also on the differential policing of different communities – the so-called 'disproportionality' debate – with important implications for criminal justice and community relations (Miller et al., 2001). Neither are the consequences of disproportionality insignificant, with the Brixton riots directly attributed by Lord Scarman to excessive stop and search operations in the minority ethnic community (Miller et al., 2001). This disproportionality debate can be illustrated by a consideration of cannabis. One of the most interesting recent developments regarding the prevalence and policing of drug use has been the challenge which has arisen from changing patterns of cannabis use in the UK and resulting tensions in the relationship between legislation, enforcement policy and practice, government position and the views of the electorate.

The 1990s saw an upsurge in involvement with cannabis, evident in the official statistics, in the British Crime Survey and in a range of local and national self-report studies. For example, persons found guilty, cautioned, fined or compounded for cannabis-related offences doubled in a decade from 40,000 in 1990 to 77,000 in 2000, with the most recent figures showing nearly 83,000 cannabis offenders in 2002 (Ahmad and Mwenda, 2004). In the British Crime Survey, self-reported lifetime prevalence of cannabis use amongst 16–29-year-olds living in private households rose by nearly a third within just six years, from 34 per cent in 1994 (Ramsay and Percy, 1996) to 44 per cent in 2000 (Ramsay et al., 2001). The most recent figures show that 26 per cent of 16–24-year-olds (an estimated 1.5 million) reported having had cannabis within the past year (Condon and Smith, 2003).

If we look in more detail at those who have been convicted of drug-related offences, there is a clear predominance of young men and those from minority ethnic communities disproportionate to their representation in the general population. The largest age category of drug offender in the official statistics in 1990–2002 is those aged 17–20 (Corkery, 2002; Ahmad and Mwenda, 2004). Further, the criminal statistics show that across the last decade men were approximately nine times more likely to get caught up in the criminal justice system for drug-related offences than women. Of those found guilty, cautioned, fined or compounded for drug offences, in 1990–2002 the percentage of female drug offenders ranged between just 8.9 per cent and 11.1 per cent in the 12-year period (Corkery, 2002; Ahmad and Mwenda, 2004). For black offenders, Home Office figures widely reported in the UK showed that for the 12 months to April 2001 black people were seven times more likely to be stopped and searched than white people, an increase from being five times more likely in the previous year (Burrell and Goodchild, 2002). Compared with approximately 5.5 per cent of the general population being minority ethnic, 12 per cent of those cautioned for drugs offences and 16 per cent of those arrested for drugs offences in 1999/2000 were minority ethnic (Home Office, 2000).

One might conclude that drug-related convictions accurately reflect those engaged in drug use in the UK if we did not further scrutinise alternative sources of information to the official statistics. A consideration of the British Crime Survey and a range of national and local self-report studies suggest that both gender and ethnic differences in drug use are somewhat different to that implied by a consideration of the official statistics alone. The 2000 British Crime Survey found that 56 per cent of 16–29-year-old men and 44 per cent of young women reported lifetime prevalence of use of any drug, providing a gender ratio of 1.3 males to 1 female, much closer than the 9:1 gender ratio in the official statistics throughout the 1990s and early 2000s. Similarly for 16–29-year- olds, 52 per cent of white respondents compared with 37 per cent of black respondents reported lifetime prevalence of use of any drug, thus providing an ethnic ratio of 1.4 white respondents to 1 black respondent in the national household survey (Ramsay et al., 2001), whereas the official statistics show black people being seven times more likely to be stopped and searched than white people. Despite the ratio of white people to black people in the general population aged 10 and over being over fifty to one and despite the British Crime Survey indicating higher self-reported drug use among the white population, the ratio of white people to black people of those stopped and searched for drugs is under 8 to 1 (Home Office, 2000).

A similar story exists for other self-report studies. Regarding gender, the north west longitudinal study found that 62 per cent of 18-year-old females and 67 per cent of males reported lifetime prevalence of use of any drug with no statistically significant gender difference (Parker et al., 1998). Regarding ethnicity, 24 per cent of 14–25-year-old black respondents compared with 37 per cent of white respondents reported lifetime prevalence of use of any drug (Graham and Bowling, 1995). Thus self-report studies raise the question of why, contrary to indications given by the official statistics, gender and ethnic differences in prevalence of drug use are not profound. Even so, this is not to suggest that there are no gender or ethnic differences in the more detailed profiles and patterns of illicit drug use. (For a discussion of gender and drugs see, for example, Henderson (1999), Measham (2002) and Ettorre (2004). For a discussion of ethnicity and drugs see, for example, Khan (1999), Murji (1999) and Fountain et al. (2004).)

While it could be argued that some gender and ethnic differences exist due to patterns of self-reporting behaviour (for example, underreporting of drug use by white men in self-report studies might explain at least part of the apparent discrepancy between self-reported cannabis use and cannabis offenders in the official statistics), research which analyses the urine of a sample of those arrested and taken to police stations (not necessarily for drug-related offences) in the UK provides further evidence regarding the selective enforcement of the cannabis laws. The positive urine tests by arrestees for cannabis add to the discrepancies in the disproportionality debate, with 49 per cent of male arrestees compared with 25 per cent of females testing positive for cannabis (a gender ratio of 2:1) and 59 per cent of non white arrestees compared with 44 per cent of white arrestees testing positive for cannabis (an ethnicity ratio of 1.3 non-white arrestees to 1 white arrestee) (Bennett, 1998). Urine analyses therefore support the findings of self-report studies of cannabis which suggest that gender and ethnic differences in official statistics are disproportionate to the prevalence of use in the general population and therefore the implementation and enforcement of the drug laws becomes a cause for concern.

Differential enforcement and the role of the criminal law

By considering the gender and ethnic ratios in these different sources of information on cannabis, it is possible to conclude that the implementation of the 1971 Misuse of Drugs Act disproportionately nets certain sections of the British population in the criminal justice system, such as young men and those from minority ethnic communities, with consequent criminal convictions and the possible future disadvantages that convictions can entail. This selective implementation of a law which attempts to control or criminalise a widespread 'deviant' behaviour such as cannabis use operates through various mechanisms, including the practice of stop and search under the Police and Criminal Evidence Act 1999, with concerns having been expressed regarding its disproportionate use in low-income, inner-city and minority ethnic communities. In stop and search cases in the Metropolitan police area, for example, drugs were the grounds given for 50 per cent of searches and for 42 per cent of arrests, with large numbers of young black and young Asian men arrested for possession of very small amounts of cannabis (FitzGerald, 1999). Although it is difficult to assess, it appears that black people (and increasingly young Asians) are more likely to be stopped, searched and arrested than white people.[2] It has been in part due to the lack of commitment of local communities to the enforcement of minor cannabis possession charges, police concerns at implementation of a law which was not a priority for the public in terms of policing and alternative pressures on police resources which led to legislative reform in the form of the reclassification of cannabis as a Class C controlled drug in 2004 after over thirty years as a Class B drug under the 1971 Misuse of Drugs Act.[3]

The example of cannabis reclassification raises questions about the role of criminal law in society and its relationship to changing patterns of criminal, 'deviant' or socially unacceptable behaviour. Clearly a criminal behaviour cannot be decriminalised or removed from the penal code simply because a large number of people engage in it, as shop theft (Kivivuori, 1998) and other crimes are committed by large numbers of people at some point in their lives. However, if the numbers engaging in a criminal behaviour grow in inverse relationship to the commitment of either the general population and/or the police to enforce that law, then legislative change might be considered.

In the case of cannabis, increased experimentation and use throughout the 1990s was accompanied by a growing accommodation or acceptance by both users and non-users, leading to a willingness to consider legislative change among the general population (Pearson and Shiner, 2002) and the police (Travis, 2000; Ellison, 2004). Such attitudinal and behavioural change occurred at a time of increased pressures on public service funding and a perceived need to prioritise aspects of policing with the estimated financial costs of policing cannabis amounting to over £50 million per annum (May et al., 2002). The general public began to rate the prosecution of cannabis-related offences as very low on their list of policing priorities compared with issues such as drink driving, alcohol-related disorder, antisocial behaviour and other concerns. The differences between these concerns are considerable. So, for example, in a Mori poll of 1,645 16–59-year-olds commissioned by the Independent Inquiry into the Misuse of Drugs Act known as the Runciman Report (Police Foundation, 2000) under 0.5 per cent thought cannabis users should be a policing priority compared with 32 per cent thinking drink driving should be a policing priority. Furthermore, only 34 per cent thought cannabis was harmful or very harmful, whereas 84 per cent thought tobacco was harmful or very harmful and 67 per cent thought alcohol was harmful or very harmful (Pearson and Shiner, 2002).

Nevertheless, some unease has been expressed at the appropriateness of the police setting an agenda for legislative reform without necessarily having an electoral mandate, a consensus among the general population[4] or indeed government support.[5] Furthermore, with 73 per cent of all drugs offenders being cannabis offenders, with 48 per cent of cannabis resin seizures and 64 per cent of herbal cannabis seizures being for amounts smaller than one gram in weight, with 77 per cent of unlawful possession offences and 97 per cent of unlawful production offences being for cannabis in 2002 (Ahmad and Mwenda, 2004), there is a further discrepancy between the professed government commitment to prioritise Class A drug use and supply (as outlined in its drug strategy of 2002) and the operation of British drug law in practice.

The 'normalisation' debate

A key debate over the last ten years within the drugs field has centred on the significance of recreational drug use, both in terms of the nature of changing patterns of recreational use of drugs such as cannabis, amphetamines, ecstasy and cocaine and the broader socio-cultural significance, with South suggesting that the case can be made that 'the dominant theme in the late modern, end-of-20th century story about drugs is a move towards "normalisation"' (1999: 6). This so-called normalisation debate has exercised drug researchers throughout the 1990s (e.g. Coffield and Gofton, 1994; Measham et al., 1994; Parker et al., 1998) and continues to do so (e.g. Parker et al., 2002; Blackman, 2004).

Proponents of normalisation suggest that the UK is in the process of major change in relation to drug-related attitudes and behaviours, with evidence of recreational drug use moving from its previously marginal, subcultural or 'deviant' status towards being widespread, acknowledged and accommodated by both users and non-users in mainstream adolescent (Parker et al., 1998), young adult (Measham et al., 2001) and adult (Pearson, 2001) society. Some have doubted the scale and significance of changes in drug-related attitudes and behaviours in the UK (e.g. Shiner and Newburn, 1997), although these early critiques have been largely surpassed by the growing body of empirical research to the contrary (e.g. Duff, 2005; Sanders, 2005).

For proponents of normalisation, however, increased psychoactive drug use and increased cultural accommodation of drug use is understood as just one symptom of major socio-economic and cultural change across the Western world. It is argued that the supply and use of drugs cannot be considered in isolation from the broader context of rapid change in late modern consumer society across the last twenty years or so. Changes such as the 'extension' of adolescence; increased uncertainties on the road to full adulthood associated with financial dependence and debt; delayed marriage, mortgage and parenthood; the changing nature of leisure and 'time out'; the changing relationship between the body, technology and medical intervention; while living in a high-risk, high-surveillance society against a backdrop of global socio-economic change and increasingly complex international criminal organisations *must* all impact on illicit drug use and supply (Parker et al., 1998; Pavis et al., 1998; Brain, 2000; Denscombe, 2001; Young, 2003; Hayward, 2004).

The process of normalisation – the accommodation of a minority behaviour by the majority – can, of course, work in both directions. It is not only the prohibited drugs under the 1971 Misuse of Drugs Act which reflect the historically and culturally changing nature of criminal, 'deviant' or socially unacceptable behaviour. There is evidence of considerable and sometimes surprising changes in attitudes towards the recreational use of legal drugs, such as tobacco and alcohol. Within the lifetime of readers of this book, the degree of socio-cultural and legal accommodation of tobacco has shifted, with increasingly controlled usage or denormalisation (Parker, 2001). After a century of widespread accommodation, tobacco has become increasingly less tolerated by the non-smoking majority across the developed world in the twenty-first century, with restrictions on smoking having been introduced, enhanced or planned in public buildings, on public transport and in leisure venues in many major cities. Interestingly, countries have varied in their response. In 2003 New York City became the first city in the world to introduce a smoking ban in public buildings such as bars and restaurants, followed by Ireland which in 2004 became the first country in the world to introduce a nationwide ban on smoking in the workplace (including pubs, clubs, theatres, restaurants, offices and even haulage vehicles). The British government has chosen a different response, however. In 2004 the UK saw the establishment of a handful of non-smoking public houses in cities such as Manchester, but to date the government continues to resist a nationwide ban (called for by the British Medical Association, the Chief Medical Officer and the leaders of all 18 royal colleges of medicine), choosing instead the more gradual development of no smoking areas through voluntary self-regulation by the hospitality and tobacco industries.

At the crime/leisure/health interface, research suggests that the use of psychoactive drugs such as tobacco persists, despite the known health risks, the increasingly aggressive public health campaigns and the increased restrictions on social smoking. Reasons for smoking in the face of known health risks include its use as a coping strategy (e.g. Graham, 1989, 1994; Graham and Blackburn, 1998); as a pleasurable pursuit (Ettorre, 1992; Henderson, 1999); as part of the construction, presentation and affirmation of the self to others during the uncertainties of contemporary times (Denscombe, 2001); as an assertion of individuality and independence in the face of the so-called health fascism of the medical establishment and paternalistic or puritanical government; and most broadly, in defiance of the universal inevitability of mortality (Cronin, 2004).[6]

In the passive smoking debate the tensions between the role of the state, the corporate responsibilities of industry, and individual rights and responsibilities are highlighted in terms of actions which may result in harm to the individual, to others and/or to wider society. Tobacco too raises the question of free will in drug use, of agency and of addiction in that smokers can be portrayed as either victims of the tobacco manufacturing industry and their consequent addiction (Gilbert and Warburton, 2000) or as champions of individual freedom and the pleasures of the 'divine Lady Nicotine' which Hilton has shown date back to nineteenth-century bourgeois traditions (2000).

One final point is that the reality of new generations of smokers, as well as drinkers, becoming regular users suggests that the perceived positive aspects of the consumption of these legal drugs and the associated lifestyle outweighs the by now widely known harmful effects to users' health. This has led public health campaigners to direct their energies towards warning young women in particular of the harmful consequences to their appearance rather than their health in a crude attempt to deter usage of legal and illicit drugs. In both the United States and the UK the police issued a series of photographs of specific individual female drug users taken when arrested throughout their adult drug-using careers as a shock campaign aimed at illustrating the negative impact of drugs on these women's looks over the course of several years (Cowan, 2004). However, the effectiveness of these national high-profile public health campaigns and local drug education campaigns in limiting or preventing drug use, whether of legal or illicit drugs, is suspect, illustrating the limitations of demand reduction policies (e.g. Dorn and Murji, 1992; Foxcroft et al., 1997; Brown and Kreft, 1998; Aldridge et al., 1999; Caulkins et al., 1999).

Policy responses to changing patterns of consumption

Policy responses to changing patterns of consumption span a broad range of possibilities from ultra prohibition with no permitted medical usage at one end (e.g. ecstasy as Class A Schedule 1 from 1977 in the UK) to complete legalisation and unrestricted sale and use at the other (e.g. caffeine). In between is a range of options – including limited prohibition, deregulation, depenalisation or reclassification, decriminalisation and controlled or licensed legalisation – which are in operation in different countries around the world and within the European Union (Dorn and Jamieson, 2000). Even in the UK drug policy is an issue which divides the main political parties and has no clear left–right alliances. While the Conservative Party is traditionally seen as the party of law and order, some on the right take a libertarian stance in favour of either legalisation of some or all illicit drugs, or of substantial reform of the 1971 Misuse of Drugs Act. One of the most surprising advances in drug-related public health in recent times was under the Conservative Prime Minister Margaret Thatcher, who faced the impending HIV/AIDS pandemic of the mid-1980s by authorising a radical public information and harm minimisation programme which facilitated needle exchange programmes for injecting drug users to reduce the potential spread of HIV/AIDS. The Labour Party could be expected to take a more reformist stance towards drug policy and a more sympathetic approach to the drug-related problems of those living on the margins of society. However, the establishment of the (New) Labour government from 1997 onwards heralded a renewed prioritisation of criminal justice rather than public health interventions as part of its 'tough on crime' as well as 'tough on the causes of crime' stance (Stimson, 2001).

Whether problematic drug use is considered primarily a criminal, health or social problem determines policy and treatment at national and local level. While it may be an oversimplification to characterise government drug policy as a pendulum swaying between criminal justice and health interventions, changes in government priorities provide an indication of attitudes to crime and social problems, to the control and criminalisation of youth and to those facing unemployment, poverty, illness and despair. As with some of the most serious crime problems faced in society, such as persistent sex offences and child abuse, it raises the question of the purpose of policy, of whether a humane and civilised society is primarily concerned with the punishment and/or treatment of those individuals engaging in socially unacceptable, 'deviant' or criminal behaviour, or whether the primary concern is to prevent such behaviours and protect the wider society from their repercussions.

Criminal justice and public health interventions

Heroin best illustrates the relationship between public health and criminal justice interventions which has characterised British drug policy over the last hundred years. The history of heroin in the UK shows how it moved from being a widely available over-the-counter remedy in the form of opium-derived products to its restricted status with the 1868 Pharmacy Act, the 1916 Defence of the Realm Act, and then to the medical profession and the Home Office developing what became known as the 'British system' after the 1926 Rolleston report (Berridge, 1980, 1981, 1984; Strang and Gossop, 1994). From 1926 to 1967, pharmaceutical grade heroin was available on prescription to the small numbers of patients who came forward with heroin dependency in a system which gave considerable autonomy to GPs to treat addicts within a framework regulated by the Home Office. However, the 1967 Dangerous Drugs Act, 1968 Medicines Act, and 1971 Misuse of Drugs Act reduced access to prescription heroin to a small number of Home Office licensed doctors and specialist clinics. The increased restrictions on heroin from the late 1960s led to a shift from medical supplies to illicit street supplies in the early 1970s, with the issues of purity, adulteration and criminal supply chains illustrating the disadvantages of a supply reduction drug policy which was successful only in reducing the supply of legitimately manufactured drugs. (For a discussion of the effectiveness of recent supply-side interventions see Benson et al. (2001), Best et al. (2001) and May and Hough (2001).)

One such policy response to the perceived 'sickness' of addiction has been the use of substitution programmes to prevent the onset of physical withdrawal symptoms through the provision of a prescription alternative, and with the broader aim of either reducing pharmacological dependence through a planned withdrawal programme or providing stability and contact with health professionals through a long-term maintenance programme. In relation to heroin, once prescription heroin was severely curtailed, the substitute most widely used in the UK became methadone. Supporters argue that it allows a controlled drug regime to be administered by trained medical professionals and thus reduces the likelihood of the many problems for both individual drug users and wider society associated with dependent and daily use of adulterated and costly street drugs. Among the problems are the daily cycle of attempting to find illicit supplies, the risks of purchasing impure street drugs and using contaminated injecting equipment, the possible reliance on acquisitive crime to fund drug use, and the wider drug-oriented lifestyle which may include risk-taking or health threatening behaviour such as unprotected sex.

Those less enamoured by methadone substitution programmes (e.g. Newcombe, 1996; Fitzpatrick, 2001) have argued that, firstly, the properties of the substitute drug may be as problematic as the primary drug of addiction (with typical annual methadone mortality rates of over two hundred per annum in the UK) and a recognised withdrawal syndrome which may be considered at least equally as intense, prolonged and traumatic as heroin. Secondly, the extent to which acquisitive crime is directly motivated by the desire to fund drug use may have been exaggerated for political purposes. Thirdly, there are limitations inherent in substitution programmes which treat the symptom (drug use) rather than the underlying causes of addiction (poverty, unemployment, social exclusion, mental illness and so forth). Fourthly, for some there is a general objection to replacing one pharmacological addiction with another.

Whether or not daily, dependent or problematic use can be considered physical, psychological, criminal or moral weakness is an area of political, philosophical and scientific debate. Indeed the nature and essence of addiction to individual drugs has filled fiction and non-fiction for centuries (e.g. Plant, 1999), with a culture of addiction resulting in the image of compulsion powerfully embedded in late modern consumer society (e.g. Cronin, 2004) and theories of addiction vigorously challenged in the field of drugs (e.g. Orford, 1985; Booth Davies, 1992).

The drugs–crime relationship

The role of drugs in crime causation is a regular feature of public and political debate and a central tenet of UK drug policy. The three main aspects of the drugs–crime nexus are, firstly, that the possession and supply of controlled psychoactive substances are offences in themselves under the 1971 Misuse of Drugs Act and its subsequent amendments; secondly, the possibility that drug dependency can lead to acquisitive crime to fund the purchase of drugs; and thirdly, that the profits from crime in general can contribute to a hedonistic consumption-oriented lifestyle which may include alcohol, tobacco and illicit drugs. In particular, a substantial amount of acquisitive crime in the UK is alleged to be motivated by the desire to raise funds for daily and dependent use of drugs such as heroin, crack, cocaine, amphetamines and alcohol. The evidence base for this economic-compulsive model of drugs causing crime has been challenged, however, by some studies which suggest that only a small proportion of the overall numbers of the drug-using population are actively engaged in criminal careers to fund their drug use and for many of these, their criminal careers preceded their problematic drug use (e.g. Brain et al., 1998; Korf et al., 1998). A far greater number of offenders who routinely use illicit drugs may or may not use the proceeds of crime to fund their drug use but this does not mean that drug use is necessarily the primary motivation for their offending (Hammersley et al., 2003). There are also significant associations between drug markets and other illicit markets, organised crime, violence and firearms offences (Bean, 2004).

Research on dance drug use, however, has challenged the traditional criminological emphasis on the drugs–crime relationship discussed above by drawing attention to the recreational use of illicit substances that may not necessarily be problematic for the individual or society beyond the illegality of possession and supply. Not only has dance drugs research de-emphasised the relationship between drugs and crime while highlighting the relationship between drugs, leisure and consumption practices, it has challenged the public and political discourses of 'mad, sad or bad' drug users caught in a trap of dependency poverty and social exclusion, a focus of earlier research (e.g. Parker et al., 1988). While the achievement of dance drug research was to recognise issues of empowerment, identity and pleasure in recreational drug use (e.g. Henderson, 1993; Redhead, 1993; Shapiro, 1999; Hinchliff, 2001), contemporary drug research is now reconsidering the binary polarisation of problematic/recreational by exploring a spectrum of drug-related profiles and behaviours which may or may not be problematic and which may or may not be related to crime (e.g. Measham et al., 2001; Simpson, 2003) and the broader agency-structure debate (e.g. Measham, 2004c).

Recreational use of drugs

It appears that recreational use of illicit drugs such as amphetamines, LSD, ecstasy and cocaine has peaked among the young adult population in the UK, at least for the time being (Condon and Smith, 2003). Although the reasons for this apparent recent reduction in self-reported drug use and numbers of seizures and offenders are at present unclear, it may be that after a decade of considerable increases in self-reported use of a range of illicit drugs across the UK across the 1990s (Ramsay et al., 2001), we might expect use to reach a plateau. Potential use may have reached saturation point with about one in twenty young adults being occasional recreational Class A drug users and about one in forty being regular monthly recreational Class A drug users, or it may tail off with a resurgence in the use of different legal and illicit psychoactive drugs such as alcohol, magic mushrooms and crack, or the use of 'new' psychoactive substances such as ketamine and 2C-B (Measham, 2004a; Miles and Moore, 2004). The broader point is that changing patterns of legal and illicit drug use, the peaks and troughs of individual drugs echoed in the British Crime Survey, the Home Office official statistics on drug seizures and offenders and in a range of self-report studies cannot be understood in isolation from each other. As noted in Measham (2004a), drug supply and use is a response not only to price, purity, access and availability but also to legislation, government policy, enforcement priorities, licensing legislation and beverage alcohol and leisure industry developments.

Alcohol is the most widely used psychoactive drug in the UK and has enormous crime and criminological implications regarding its perceived relationship to violence, disorder, antisocial behaviour and a wide range of alcohol-related crimes (e.g. Deehan, 1999). While there is undoubtedly an association between alcohol and crime, the precise nature of the relationship and its cultural significance as part of a particularly British 'binge and brawl' culture is subject to persistent debate (e.g. Sumner and Parker, 1995). There is not the space to discuss this debate in detail; however, two points of relevance are noted here in relation to wider criminological discussion on, firstly, the regulation and policing of pleasure and, secondly, interagency collaboration in response to crime problems.

Policing pleasure

The UK has a long history of not only alcohol-based leisure but also public and political anxieties about attendant alcohol-related disorder (e.g. Pearson, 1983). While northern European and particularly British alcohol consumption patterns have been characterised as emphasising weekend intoxication rather than daily conviviality (e.g. Marsh and Fox Kibby, 1992), increased concerns have been expressed about the rise in so-called 'binge drinking' (e.g. Engineer et al., 2003). Increased sessional consumption of alcohol by young people has been evident in the UK since the mid-1990s resulting from a combination of factors which have included the marketing of new high strength flavoured alcoholic beverages (McKeganey et al., 1996; McKeganey, 1998; Measham, 2004b), alongside the redesign of traditional pubs into twenty-first century café bars as part of a velvet revolution in licensed leisure – in part in response to the popularity of the 1990s dance drug and dance club scene – which revitalised urban night-time economies (Measham, 1996; Collin and Godfrey, 1997; Hobbs et al., 2000). This revolution in licensed leisure has recently led to growing concerns about alcohol being the biggest drug problem the UK faces, leading to a combination of (sometimes conflicting) responses from government departments such as the Department for Culture, Media and Sport (DCMS), the Department of Health and the Home Office.

Interagency collaboration?

The DCMS is supporting the implementation of the government's 2003 Licensing Act (with implementation currently planned for November 2005), which will continue the process of liberalisation of licensing restrictions for licensed leisure venues selling alcohol which started in the 1980s, to facilitate staggered closing times which the government hopes will encourage a more relaxed drinking culture. Phil Burke, spokesperson for Manchester's Pub and Club Network, said of the Licensing Act that 'we fully support and welcome the new 24-hour licensing reforms. They will help stagger the number of people pouring on to our city streets at the same time every night, and will also stop people from rushing from bar to bar binge-drinking' (Ducker, 2004). As Burke recognises, the rationale behind the recent legislation is that the relaxation of licensing laws will facilitate a more leisurely pace of alcohol consumption akin to the southern European style without the frenzied drinking, drunkenness and disorder evident in and around licensed leisure venues at weekends in the UK (e.g. Gofton, 1990; Marsh and Fox Kibby, 1992). There are two concerns in relation to this: firstly, the legislation has been criticised as a simplistic solution to a complex and long-standing cultural problem with some doubt about the pace or even possibility by which an embedded tradition of human behaviour can be modified. Secondly, the evidence base for the legislation has been called into question with the experience of Ireland, Australia and New Zealand cited as examples whereby similar policies which liberalised licensing laws resulted in an increase rather than decrease in drunkenness, disorder and violence and consequently licensing restrictions were reimposed.

By contrast, the Home Office is under considerable pressure to reduce alcohol-related problems associated with the perceived increase in 'binge' drinking and antisocial behaviour in the night-time economy, with concerns expressed that extended licences will exacerbate law and order problems (Richardson and Budd, 2003). The long-standing 'problem' of youth has led to increased control and criminalisation of low-level criminal and 'deviant' behaviour on the streets most recently through extensive CCTV surveillance, curfew orders, antisocial behaviour orders, by-laws allowing police seizure of alcohol in public places, the introduction of Street Crime Wardens in cities such as Manchester, and so forth. This transformation in what, where and when people drink (Measham, 2004b) is also at odds with Department of Health guidelines on sensible drinking levels and the recent high profile launch of the alcohol harm reduction strategy by the Prime Minister's Strategy Unit (2004). This current dilemma for the Home Office, the DCMS and the Department of

Health illustrates a key challenge for coordinated multi-agency responses to the regulation and management of illicit and legal drug use.

The question of corporate responsibility in advertising, marketing, licensing and product development for legal drugs, in the maintenance and management of licensed leisure locations and the health and safety of customers is a further issue for consideration. Partnerships between the beverage alcohol industry, public health community, researchers and the government can potentially focus on areas of common concern such as the reduction of alcohol-related problems, while also promoting the long-standing positive role of alcohol in British leisure in terms of facilitating social interaction, celebration and ceremony (Peele and Grant, 1999). The beverage alcohol industry has stated its commitment to encouraging responsible drinking through the Dublin Principles (1997) ('Only the legal and responsible consumption of alcohol should be promoted by the beverage alcohol industry and others involved in the production, sale, regulation, and consumption of alcohol') and the Geneva Partnership (2000). Building on the Dublin Principles and the result of over two years of meetings and the input of over 200 individuals to develop public/ private sector partnership in alcohol policy worldwide, the 2000 Geneva Partnership was formulated as a policy tool to assist alcohol policy development at the national and international level.[7]

However, there is a credibility gap here between the professed corporate responsibility of the legal drugs industries and the capitalist imperative of the market. Alcohol researchers in the UK and elsewhere find no shortage of licensed leisure premises willing to serve customers far more than the UK recommended daily 'sensible' drinking levels of four units of alcohol for men and three units for women, and the continuation of marketing and promotion strategies of concern to public health and criminal justice bodies (e.g. 2 for 1, happy hours, free drinks for limited time period, loyalty card schemes and so forth). Any serious commitment by the beverage alcohol industry to ensuring that alcohol consumption levels remain within the guidelines for sensible daily recommended intake would result in turning away an awful lot of custom.

Conclusion

This chapter has discussed some key issues in the field of drug and alcohol studies, which reflect and reinforce the wider debates within criminology represented elsewhere in this collection.

Like criminology, the field of drugs is multidisciplinary in outlook and multi-method in research design and as a specialist subject can tease out theoretical, methodological, empirical and policy issues within and across the social science disciplines, growing both as a specialist sub-discipline of criminology and as a subject in its own right. The aim of this chapter has been to show just a few of the ways in which the world of drugs (and thus the field) has changed enormously not only in relation to patterns of use but also legislation, enforcement, treatment and theoretical and policy developments, resulting in the emergence of a distinct and important area of concern for the twenty-first century.

It is in the discrepancies between different studies and sources of information on drug-related behaviours that we can see the selective policing, targeting and enforcement of drug legislation and the impact of implementation on communities. The importance of social and structural factors such as gender, ethnicity and poverty help our understanding not only of criminal, 'deviant' or antisocial behaviour but also of the processes of prohibition, the policing of such behaviours and the organisations or spheres of power influencing these processes. Moreover, research on drugs provides an indicator of the historically, culturally and socially context-specific nature of any country's attitudes to crime and deviance at any one moment, directly linked to contemporary politics, international criminal organisations, the story of nation states and of migration, of relations between the developed and developing world and the policing of minority ethnic communities across the world. For example, the historically and culturally context-specific nature of what behaviour is deemed criminal or 'deviant' in society and what behaviour is condoned or accepted is well illustrated by the changing legal status of different psychoactive drugs across the centuries.

Drug policy illustrates central debates within criminology regarding the tensions between principle and pragmatism in the design and implementation of legislation and in whether the aims of legislation are crime prevention or minimising the harm to society and/or to the individual from a particular behaviour. Furthermore, the aims, implications and consequences of drug policy raise questions about crime causation, the development of criminal careers, the type of society we desire and treating problem behaviour either through prioritising criminal or medical interventions, at the heart of which is the persistent 'mad, sad or bad' political discourse. In British drug policy it has been suggested that there has been a long-standing accommodation between public health, criminal and other policy initiatives for broad-ranging political and practical reasons.

Drug policy determines the treatment of some of the most vulnerable and marginal in any society and as such is also an indicator of the degree of compassion or humanity in that society. Moreover, drug consumption itself presents a powerful and persistent sign of the continuing human search for ways to maximise pleasure and minimise pain. The legal status of psychoactive drugs defines the boundaries of criminality, normality and deviance, of the acceptability of social regulation and state criminalisation. When teaching drug and alcohol studies at undergraduate and postgraduate level, a reflection on definitions of criminality and deviance becomes all the more significant when over half of the students on any given course in this field are likely to have engaged in the criminal behaviour under consideration and almost all will have direct contact with family, friends and colleagues who have tried drugs.

Notes

1   The term 'drugs' is used in this chapter to denote psychoactive substances consumed without medical authorisation or prescription, regardless of the legal status of these drugs. The term illicit is used here to refer to both illegal drugs, i.e. those drugs controlled under the 1971 Misuse of Drugs Act and its subsequent amendments (e.g. heroin, ecstasy, cannabis and cocaine), and quasi-legal drugs, i.e. those drugs not totally prohibited but whose possession, supply, manufacture or preparation is partially prescribed in some way in British law (e.g. alkyl nitrites, solvents).

2   Home Office figures show that people of minority ethnic origin are more likely to be stopped and searched disproportionately to their representation in the general population: 8 per cent of people stopped and searched in 1999/2000 were of black ethnic origin compared to 2 per cent aged 10 and over in the general population, 4 per cent of those stopped and searched were Asian compared to 3 per cent in the general population, and 85 per cent of those stopped and searched were white compared to 95 per cent in the general population. Home Office figures also show that people of minority ethnic origin are more likely to be stopped and searched for drug offences. Of black people stopped and searched in England and Wales in 1999/2000 under PACE, 41 per cent were for suspected drugs offences. Of Asian people stopped and searched, 52 per cent were for suspected drugs offences. Of white people stopped and searched, 30 per cent were for suspected drugs offences (Home Office, 2000). The significance of this was noted by the Runciman Report (Police Foundation, 2000: chapter 7, no. 75).

3   Further evidence of the selective enforcement of drug laws having a detrimental impact on minority ethnic communities can be found in the historical development of the heroin trade route to the United States after the Second World War. Reflected in films such as *Lucky Luciano* (1971), *The Godfather* (1972) and *The French Connection* (1973) (Viano, 2002), heroin was manufactured in Italy and was transported to the United States via Marseilles. Heroin became particularly associated with the black African American community in the postwar period because the Mafia at that time concentrated sales specifically in those neighbourhoods. It has been suggested that the reason why the Italian Mafia was able to traffick in heroin with relative ease from Italy to France and then on to the USA was because of American officials'

willingness to 'overlook' this trade in recognition of, firstly, Sicilian Mafia support for the Allied invasion of Sicily in the Second World War and, secondly, French and Corsican Mafia assistance against the communist trade unions (Viano, 2002).

4   A *Guardian*/ICM poll published in the *Guardian* on 17 October 2000 reported that 43 per cent of voters thought personal use of cannabis should be completely legalised.

5   A leader comment in the *Observer* newspaper noted that 'we cannot feel entirely comfortable with radical legislative changes being decided in the police canteen' (25 November 2001). See also the autobiographical account of the political background to cannabis depenalisation by Keith Hellawell, ex-drug Czar (2002), and reflections on the 'farce of cannabis re-classification' by the former Detective Chief Superintendant at Scotland Yard Central Drug Squad (Ellison, 2004: 419).

6   The printing of stern health warnings about the dangers of smoking on packets of cigarettes has led to novel ways to avoid or subvert them. Some Spanish smokers have evaded the health warnings on packets of cigarettes by either decanting their cigarettes into traditional cigarette cases (some of which have been designed to look identical to packets of branded cigarettes but without the health warnings) or by covering up health warnings on standard cigarette packets using special stickers carrying alternative messages such as 'Living is fatal' (Tremlett, 2003).

7   Regarding advertising and promotion the Geneva Partnership says that 'beverage alcohol industry members should promote only the responsible consumption of their products and should not encourage irresponsible or inappropriate consumption' (2000).

Chapter 7

Explaining changing patterns of crime: a focus on burglary and age–period–cohort models

Brian Francis and Keith Soothill

Introduction

Politicians and the media seem to have little difficulty in focusing upon changing patterns of crime. They reflect nostalgically on a golden past when there was supposedly little crime. They point to an earlier period – usually the 1960s – which they see as acting as a seedbed for current problems. They talk of young people being out of control and lacking the discipline of earlier generations. Sensational headlines abound. In contrast, criminologists seem much more reticent when considering changing patterns of crime. Such caution may well arise out of the difficulties attached to methodology and data analysis that can make theorising about change a complex activity.

The focus of this chapter is on the analysis of changing patterns of crime, which one cannot divorce from consideration of social change in general. To explore changing patterns of crime requires clarification of some key issues: for example, what is the difference between explanation and prediction, what are the differences between age, cohort and period effects, what can be gained by the use of statistical modelling and where does theorising fit in with this type of analysis? Rather than arguing that all criminologists should become highly numerate, we argue that what is needed is clear and detailed analysis of studies of change.

We explore these issues by considering two recent pieces of work concerned with crime rates. The first, the Civitas Report, relates to the allegedly increasing amount of crime, specifically burglary; and the second is an econometric model concerned with the forecasting of future burglary. Both of these will act as case studies in this chapter, providing relevant examples of how to analyse and interpret studies of change in depth. What insight can we gain into the debate on change from these two studies and how can we evaluate them to see what they actually mean in real life?

The Civitas Report on police performance

On 2 January 2005, the *Observer* reported on new research produced by the 'right-wing think-tank' Civitas (Dennis and Erdos, 2005). Under the headline 'UK Police among world's worst', the newspaper went on to say that the increase in recorded crime was, according to the researchers, 'the worst of four countries' (the others being France, Germany and the USA) and blamed this on the breakdown of the traditional family. the *Guardian*, on the following day, gave more details. They quoted the report as attributing increases in crime (such as the five-fold increase in burglaries from 72,000 in 1964 to 402,000 in 2003/4) to a moral decline resulting from the 1960s cultural revolution which has fuelled criminality. The article, however, also quoted the Police Foundation who called the report simplistic for failing to take account of the changes in reporting and recording of crime over this period, the huge change in property ownership, and the great increase in material wealth, meaning that there were more goods to steal.

We can see that the two sets of explanations being presented here are rather different in nature. Dennis and Erdos are asserting that different generations, being brought up under differing parental regimes, account for the increases in crime. This assertion is similar to that of Tony Blair who in warning that 1960s liberalism had gone too far, said that people now 'want rules, order and proper behaviour' (Blair, 2004). We can refer to this as the *generational* explanation of crime, which historically has been a right-of-centre argument. In contrast, the Police Foundation is asserting that crime varies from year to year because of factors such as changes in reporting rates and property ownership, which themselves vary from year to year and affect all generations equally. We will not attempt at this stage to referee between these two opposing views, but simply point out that any analysis which attempts to determine whether generational effects or yearly effects provide the main drivers of crime is fraught with difficulty. We will see later that this kind of issue has, similarly, been a traditional problem for epidemiologists when they confront the changing rates of disease over time. Termed 'age–period–cohort' studies, they attempt to separate out cohort (or generational) effects from period (or yearly) effects and age effects.

However, there are technical matters to consider that are often troublesome. So, for example, it is impossible to disentangle the effects of year and generation without having datasets disaggregated by age and, with longitudinal datasets, disaggregation by age allows us to begin to separate out the effect of generational factors from year factors. Thus the crucial issue is that Civitas and the Police Foundation are giving competing explanations about crime figures that are untested by any systematic analysis. While both may have strong theoretical and political reasons to take the line that they do, the debate is limited without richer data disaggregated by age which will allow greater insight into changing patterns of crime.

Before moving on to probe the econometric model, we must first mention more about the techniques used to analyse such datasets. Most importantly, we introduce the concepts of 'statistical' modelling and 'econometric' modelling.

Statistical and econometric modelling

It is clear that a simple examination of crime figures can provide little evidence in *explaining* crime. One way of proceeding, however, is to attempt to build statistical models for such crime series, which can provide evidence on which of a number of factors appear to be associated with increasing crime.

Statistical modelling is concerned with finding structure in a quantitative dataset, and in separating that structure from the noise, or random variation, which occurs in all sets of data. The structure of the model provides an assessment of association – a particular variable such as the rate of crime is associated with a collection of other explanatory variables, and these associations may provide a method of formulating and developing an explanation for why a particular effect was observed. It is important to note that a selection process among the possible explanatory variables takes place, and a good statistical model is one that is parsimonious (that is, it has as few variables as possible) as well as describing as much of the structure as possible. Unimportant measures which are not associated with the quantity of interest are excluded, and only important, associated quantities are included.

With statistical modelling examining, say, a crime series over time, our variable of interest may be the observed yearly numbers of police recorded crime. To move the analysis forward, we could seek to explain the changes in recorded crime by a variety of different measures, including the economic and social conditions, population and demographic information, criminal justice variables and some historical measures of childhood factors. From this collection, a parsimonious set of variables that are strongly associated with, say, burglary crime rates are identified, and a mathematical formula is constructed which describes that relationship. Although there are exceptions, statistical modellers would normally attempt to collect a wide range of variables which could cover a variety of different theories of crime and would 'let the data speak'. Thus, when we refer to statistical modelling here, we are talking about an atheoretical method (that is, one not based on any one theory), which is inductive in nature – the statistical model and the associations found can be used to suggest and build new theories and to challenge others.

Another approach, which is essentially an offshoot of statistical modelling, is econometric modelling. While its roots may be the same, the approach and the implications of the analysis, including the interpretation of results, are very different and criminologists need to be aware of this.

In contrast to statistical modelling, econometric modelling is concerned primarily with building *economic* explanations of phenomena using statistical modelling techniques. Typically, there would tend to be an economic theory underlying the statistical method that would tend to inform the choice of measures collected and analysed.

An econometric model of changes in burglary rates since the Second World War

Like the debate initiated by the Civitas Report, our case study is again concerned with changing crime rates over time. This time, however, the focus is specifically on the changing rates of burglary since the Second World War. This will enable us to demonstrate an example of an econometric model in action, and to highlight the fact that great care is needed when modelling data. The econometric model fails dramatically, and examining why it fails helps to probe a way forward for the future.

In 1999, Dhiri and colleagues published an account of modelling the number of all recorded burglaries in England and Wales over a 48-year period from 1951 to 1998 (Dhiri et al., 1999). This work was in turn heavily based on work by Field (1999). One of the aims of this modelling was to predict future numbers of recorded burglaries. The result – that the yearly number of reported burglaries in England and Wales would increase by 25 per cent and that for theft would increase by 40 per cent over a three-year period to 2001 – proved highly controversial and attracted much press coverage and academic comment, much of it critical.

If we probe further into the methodology, we discover that an econometric model was used to produce the forecasts. Econometric models of crime have sometimes been justified by rational choice theory – that is, theory based on the idea that individuals commit crime where the net gain (the gain from the crime minus the loss from the possibility of being apprehended) is positive. However, the authors of the burglary report followed Field (1999) in grounding the justification in routine activity theory. Indeed, in a retrospective article on this work, Harries (2003) states that the work is 'unequivocally based' on routine activities theory. Thus this predictive work is based on a single theory of crime.

It is worth taking some time to examine this particular theory of criminal behaviour. Routine activities theory was first proposed by Cohen and Felson (1979) who maintained that three minimal elements are necessary for a crime to be committed – motivated offenders, suitable targets and capable guardians. However, as Bottoms and Wiles (2002: 630) stress, of the three elements identified, routine activities theory has in practice concentrated very heavily on the second and third (suitable targets and capable guardians). Nevertheless, despite largely ignoring the offender dimension, the routine activities approach has usefully developed and extended the straightforward concept of 'opportunity'. It focuses on the day-to-day activities of potential victims of crime and of those potentially able to offer 'natural surveillance', and specifically emphasises 'the fundamental human ecological character of illegal acts as *events* which occur at specific locations in *space* and *time*, involving specific persons and/or objects' (Cohen and Felson, 1979: 589, emphasis in original).

The research team considered a number of variables to measure these components of the theory, and based their choice on previous research by Field and others – 'the culmination of ten years of research and development', as Harries (2003) puts it. The variables they finally chose were a measure of consumption, a variable which they called 'stock of opportunities' and a variable representing the proportion of young men in the population. The consumption variable – assessed by total household consumption expenditure adjusted to 1995 prices – played two roles, both as a motivating factor (more consumption in the population increases an individual's expectation of wealth and decreases the risk of an individual carrying out a burglary) and also as a measure of the number of 'capable guardians': more consumption implies that property owners are away from their property more and are less able to guard it. The 'stock of opportunities' variable represented the number of stealable goods and was simply the sum of the previous four years' consumption – the idea being that goods over four years old are not worth stealing. Finally, a somewhat curious measure of young males was assessed by the sum of the estimated number of males aged 15 and the sum of the number of estimated males aged 20, and this measure supposedly represented the potential motivated offender population.

In the present case, although Dhiri and colleagues considered other, more criminologically relevant variables as alternatives or as extra variables, such as unemployment, the number of males aged 15–24 and criminal justice variables, these were mostly rejected for technical reasons. Again, this underlines the point that models will often be constructed using variables that are available rather than those that are ideal.

A complex econometric model was built which (on the logarithmic scale) predicted changes in the amount of burglary by the absolute level of burglary and changes in burglary in the previous year, the number of young men in the previous year, the stock of opportunities in the previous year and changes in the current level of consumption. The model was an 'error correction model' which assumed that there is a long-run equilibrium of crime on some scale – in this case the log scale.

Predictions were made for 1999, 2000 and 2001 – three years into the future. However, the predictions from the model could also be compared with the data used to fit the model. In fact, the decline of burglary by 5 per cent in 1998 was *not* predicted by their model, which instead estimated an increasing trend to 2001. Figure 7.1 shows the observed number of recorded burglaries and Dhiri's predicted model for 1999–2001. In their formulation, in stable economic conditions, burglary is on a relentless onward increase, and little can be done to stop it. In the event this seems both pessimistic and wrong.

A similar point has been made by other critics. Such models suggest 'possibly exponential growth in levels of property crime' (Harries, 2003). While it is fair to point out that burglary has indeed risen exponentially over the last 40 years, this should not necessarily mean that future levels will continue this trend. As we have tried to stress, change is always possible.

Four years later, the predictions made were compared with the actual recorded crime figures for burglary. Table 7.1 shows the results. The forecast shows recorded burglary in 2001 increasing to 1.24 million crimes, whereas actual recorded burglary continued to decline to 868,000.

While Dhiri et al.'s work has been subjected to a number of criticisms, it appears that few have questioned the underlying criminological theory and data on which the work is based. Criticisms have primarily been based on the form of the econometric model, that is on technical issues. We certainly must focus on these but, first, we must consider other possibilities. As every first-year criminology student knows, criminal statistics are *socially* constructed and so one needs to understand the social processes that went into their construction. Further, definitional issues are

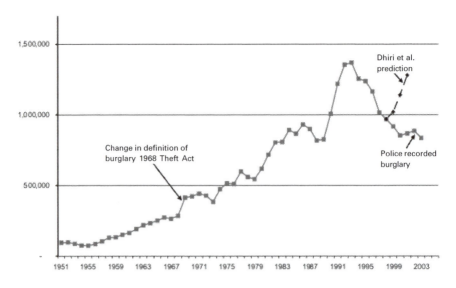

Figure 7.1 Police recorded 'All burglary' in England and Wales 1951–2003 and Dhiri et al.'s prediction for 1999–2001.

Table 7.1 Predictions 1999–2001 and actual numbers of recorded burglary 1997–2003

	Estimated predictions of number of recorded burglaries (Dhiri et al., 1999)		Actual number of recorded burglaries
1997			1,015,075
1998	970,000	(actual)	970,000
1999	1,020,000		918,000 *
2000	1,140,000		854,000 *
2001	1,280,000		868,000 *
2002			886,000 *
2003			836,000 *

*The recorded burglary figure for 1999 was produced by a weighted average of the actual number of recorded burglaries in 1998/9 and 1999/0 in the ratio ¼ : ¾. A similar procedure produced the figures for 2000–3.

often crucial – do the terms mean the same over time? Thus we now turn to focus on definitions, recorded crime and social change, and the relevance of criminological theory that criminologists need to embrace. We then return to the more technical issues that statisticians will wish to consider.

Definitions

Focusing on definitions will often seem tedious but is always essential. This is especially the case when one is considering an offence over a long time-span, for the meaning of the offence may change. Of course, this seems unlikely with burglary for this has been a clearly understood offence from time immemorial – or has it?

The work by Dhiri et al. looked at 'all burglary' – that is both domestic burglary and breaking into shops and warehouses. The domestic component of 'burglary' certainly seems non-contentious in terms of breaking into a house to steal. However, historically, there are some other interesting nuances. So, for example, burglary was defined by section 25 of the Larceny Act 1916 as breaking and entering a dwelling house and could be only committed at night between the hours of 9 p.m. and 6 a.m. (Giles, 1963). In contrast, housebreaking was not an essentially nocturnal activity and could be committed at any time and was not limited to dwelling-houses (but included shops, offices, warehouses and most kinds of shelters short of a marquee or bell tent). This all changed with the Theft Act 1968, but this helps to explain why many dictionaries still define a 'burglar' as 'one who breaks into a house *by night* to commit a felony' (emphasis added).

Certainly, examination of the number of burglaries around 1968 implies that this change in definition had a strong effect. In 1968, under the old definition, the number of recorded burglaries of all types was 285,000. In 1969, this increased dramatically to 415,000 – a 45 per cent increase. The work by Dhiri appears not to have taken account of this change in definition. So one crucial question of interest is to identify such shifts in definition.

Recorded crime and social change

Interpreting recorded crime figures is always problematic. We need to be aware that these figures are socially constructed. What this means is that the recorded burglary figures published by the Home Office cannot hope to be a true picture of the totality of burglary in England and Wales.

Firstly, not all burglary is reported – break-ins may not even be noticed, or if they are, might not be brought to the attention of the police. Victims might feel intimidated, or might feel that there is no point in reporting such crime as nothing will be done. An increasing requirement of insurance companies is that they will only pay up if the burglary is reported to the police and this will inevitably produce a higher rate of reported and recorded burglaries.

However, not all burglaries reported to the police are recorded and there have been changes in practice in this respect over time. Before 1998, every police force had considerable autonomy as to whether to record a particular crime reported to them. In 1998, new rules were introduced by the Home Office to try to standardise crime recording. The National Crime Recording Standard provides strict guidelines on when a crime should be recorded and when not, and a set of counting rules provides instruction on how many crimes are to be recorded. One crucial change is a move to a more victim-centred approach to counting – so a spree burglar who breaks into three flats in a block generates three recorded crimes rather than one. This type of change must be taken into account when time series of crime rates are considered with a range both prior to and subsequent to 1998.

Additionally, there are likely to have been earlier administrative changes at the local level that can drastically alter recorded crime. For example, the Home Office reports that following the terrorist attack on New York on September 11, 2001, the police deployed more officers in the centre of London. Following this date, there were falls in recorded burglary in Westminster in Central London and rises in Outer London in the following months (Home Office, 2002).

Thus, however good or bad police recording practices are, they only relate to crimes that are reported to officials and, hence, explain the nomenclature of '*official* statistics'. There are, however, ways of probing further and getting closer to the 'real' extent of crime or, in our case, burglary. Self-report victimisation surveys are such a mechanism. So, for example, the British Crime Survey can give a picture of the proportion of *domestic* burglary which is reported to the police. In 1980, the proportion was 66 per cent, and this has shown a slight decline since, reaching 62 per cent in the 2003/4 survey. Estimates of domestic burglary incidents can also be examined, and these provide a very similar picture to 'all burglary' recorded crime, increasing until the early 1990s and then falling steeply.

Even if one accepts the nature of the data, the extra dimension of social change produces additional difficulties. There may be more structural reasons why econometric models might fail in predicting future levels of crime. We discuss two reasons.

The first relates to social change itself. Social change will modify the behaviour of individuals and will ensure that the relationships between crime and explanatory factors are changing. Crime is a social process and is not static, and the nature of crime is continually shifting. The methods and motivations to commit crime might well be changing over a 48-year period, and the meaning of variables will also change. To take the specific example of burglary, there are many factors that can be considered as social change. There may be a supposition that the increased use of burglar alarms and other crime prevention activities have directed criminal activity away from burglary into more lucrative areas. Secondly, government policy intervenes throughout the series. To assume, as these models do, that government policy will have no effect on burglary rates is a bold assumption as well as dispiriting to politicians. Thirdly, it is likely that the characteristics of burglars have changed over the 48 years of the study. Certainly we seem to have more female burglars than yesteryear. In 2003, 7.2 per cent of convicted offenders were female, but in 1955 only 2.9 per cent were. Finally, the variable of recorded crime itself depends on social and economic factors. When the population is wealthy, then individuals are more likely to insure their property, and a burglary is more likely to be reported to the police as an insurance company requires a crime number.

The second issue, which we return to later, is that there may be generational factors at work. Burglary may simply be going out of fashion among a younger generation. Why burgle a house when drug-dealing or street robbery appears to be easier? Alternatively, perhaps there is a changing generational pattern, and offenders spend less of their life considering burglary as a lifestyle choice and move quickly onto other crimes.

One needs to recognise, then, that apparent changes in crime rates may be contingent on factors that may not be included in the model. The perennial question is whether actual offending behaviour has changed or whether official reactions to delinquency have changed. Econometricians have shown limited understanding of the implications of the social construction of official statistics or, indeed, of the relevance of social change. However, we are also concerned with their use of criminological theory.

Relevance of criminological theory

Much econometric modelling is based on *one* theory of crime – routine activities theory, or its forerunner rational choice theory. Perhaps the choice is unsurprising, as econometricians will search for theories of crime with an economic focus. Elsewhere (see Chapter 1) the dangers of general theories based on one or two variables have been stressed and here we have another variant. Concentrating on variables with an economic focus immediately limits the nature of the statistical model. Social and bio-psychological explanations are not considered.

This point was made explicitly by Field (1999: 22) in a Home Office report on crime rate trends. He stated that:

> Many factors affect crime. They may include, for example, criminal justice policy and practices, the features of parenting and childhood deprivation which precipitate delinquency, and crime prevention measures and programmes. Such factors are not amenable to this type of analysis, since they can be difficult to reflect in quantified time series.

The issues of definition, the social construction of official statistics, the dangers of relying on a few variables and just one theory are rarely confronted in an econometric approach. We now move on to the specific criticisms of the burglary model constructed by Dhiri and his colleagues.

Technical criticisms of the burglary model of Dhiri and his colleagues

Issues to be considered here relate to three components – the choice of series to be modelled, the variables used to predict the crime series and technical issues related to the statistical form of the model.

The first issue is one which, surprisingly, has not been considered by commentators. Dhiri et al. modelled the number of recorded burglaries and not the burglary rate – the numbers were *not* standardised for the population at risk. The England and Wales population grew from 43,815,000 in 1951 to 52,085,000 in 2001. Over the same period the number of households increased from 13,259,000 to 21,660,000. Such population growth needs to be taken into account when explaining numbers of recorded burglaries. A more appropriate way of proceeding is to consider burglary *rates* – the number of recorded burglaries per 1,000 households, per 1,000 population or per 1,000 adult population, and to investigate the change in such rates.

We now move on to the variables chosen to explain burglary. Deadman (2003) gently criticises Dhiri et al. (1999) for basing predictions on just three variables, and proposes additional variables relating to criminal justice.

In Deadman's model for residential burglary, unemployment and criminal justice variables measuring imprisonment, sentencing, conviction and police activity were all included, as well as a dummy variable to take account of the change in definition caused by the 1968 Theft Act. Including such variables in his analysis had the effect of reducing the estimated percentage increase of residential burglaries in future years, although substantial increases were still forecast. This suggests that in reaching a satisfactory explanation of the changing rates of burglary, there is more to tell than positing a few economic variables.

In some senses the problems of econometric models are simply the problems of statistical modelling 'writ large'. While econometric models can try hard to represent a particular view of crime through a statistical model, they are always susceptible to factors not built in and the assumptions made, such as the long-run equilibrium of crime. In addition, such models are working at a large-scale level – modelling the total crime in a large area for annual data over a period of years. Our message is that, with appropriate data, it is possible to do better. But also we are more cautious. Rather than trying to *predict* future crime, we need to obtain greater insight into *explaining* changes in crime and crime rates. To begin to explain changes in crime and crime rates more effectively, we will need to start to disaggregate even more basic variables than economic ones, namely the age and gender of offenders. This is crucial in examining change, for disaggregation by age allows us to begin to separate out the effect of generational factors from year factors.

To achieve this, one must first recognise that recorded crime figures – on which most of the analysis on changes in crime has to date been carried out – are not disaggregated by age and gender of the offender, as in many cases the offender is unknown and hence such information cannot be collected. Thus we need to move to an analysis of *offenders* – those arrested or cautioned or convicted of crime – and with all the attendant conceptual problems that such a change of focus entails. However, it is at this point that we need to recognise that others – in other disciplines – have successfully charted these troubled waters.

The medical approach to modelling rates: untangling age, period and cohort effects

In some respects, there appears to be little connection between rates of a disease and rates of crime. Indeed, there has always been concern among criminologists at seeing crime in medical terms and the dangers of the medicalisation of deviance in general has a long history. Nevertheless, our focus here is on the technical issues that epidemiologists have usefully confronted.

Epidemiologists have a similar desire to criminologists to know why rates are changing, but recognise that rates of a disease are often caused by many factors. In essence, however, these factors can be classified into effects of age, effects of period (or of year) and effects of cohort (or of generation). Let us consider a current problem that actively attracts medical concern, namely that of the rates of coronary heart disease, and consider how we can begin to disentangle these terms.

Age effects are often straightforward in epidemiology. As the body ages, individuals become more susceptible to certain diseases. However, such effects are often non-linear – that is, rates can increase strongly in early years and increase less dramatically in later life – breast cancer is an example. Coupled with this are *generational* or *cohort* effects. These relate to a whole host of factors relating to upbringing, development and attitudes of a particular generation or birth cohort. By the time an individual reaches adulthood, it is usually assumed that these are set and will influence later life. For example, there is much current concern about the fatty diets of children. It is assumed that such children will become used to such a diet and will continue eating such food for the rest of their lives. If action successfully changes the diet of a new generation of children, then the outcome will be that we will have generational differences.

Finally, we have *period* or *year* effects. These can be thought of as effects that affect everyone, young or old, living through a particular period in a similar way. For example, the introduction of a new effective cholesterol-busting drug would be a year effect – deaths from heart disease would be expected to drop for all age groups following such intervention. Introduction of a government tax on high-cholesterol foods might generate a similar but perhaps less strong year effect. Year effects could also be economic – unemployment rates might affect diet – or environmental – atmospheric pollution changes or climate changes.

We can now return to criminology. How do age, period and cohort effects translate into this area?

1 *Age* effects can be viewed, as in medicine, as a primarily biological and psychological effect. Changes in adolescence, particularly among boys, will bring about behavioural changes, involving the need for more independence, to rebel against one's parents, to become involved in risk-taking and to seek out new experiences. For many, this will lead to an increased risk of criminal behaviour. This is recognised in the classic shape of the age–crime curve, which shows an increase in the numbers involved in crime from the age of criminal responsibility (10 years) onwards, peaking at 17 or 18, and then declining slowly. In other words, this is a non-linear effect with crime rates generally increasing at certain ages rather than others.

2 In contrast, *period* effects may be the outcome of a much wider variety of variables. The effect of economic variables, such as unemployment, is easily understood, but it would be misleading to regard economic variables as the only likely period effects. Environmental effects such as the number of cars with car alarms, the effect of government policy and other year-to-year changes that will affect all age groups equally may be just as important. For example, the increased encouragement of prison as an intervention by Michael Howard, as Home Secretary, led to rises in the prison population 'across the board' during this period in the 1990s.

3 Finally, we have *cohort* or *generational* effects. These can be viewed as effects usually early on in life for an individual both in a particular year or set of years which affect all subsequent behaviour. Some cohort effects are personal to the individual, others are common to all individuals born in a particular year. So, a common effect might be that children born in wartime are likely to have had rather different

childhood experiences to peacetime children. Other effects on individual childhood upbringing can also be viewed as generational effects. A major individual cohort effect is the sex of the individual, either through biological, genetic and hormonal factors or through gender-related differences in upbringing.

How does all this relate to theories of crime and the approaches of econometricians in particular? We can now see that the econometric models for burglary proposed by both Dhiri and Deadman are strong on period effects. The variables used are primarily concerned with year-to-year measures of the criminal justice system and economic health. However, their models do not consider the possibility of generational effects. In this respect, they are somewhat limited with regard to their explanatory force and the confidence one can place on their findings.

The problems of failing to take into account age–period–cohort effects are not just a failing of econometric approaches. Other theories of crime, in contrast, may be strong on generational effects. These maintain that early childhood experiences are the primary cause of later delinquent activity. Life course theories especially focus on parental conflict, poor child-rearing and separation as major influences on subsequent criminal behaviour. Farrington (1990), for example, reports six categories of risk factor: disruptive child behaviour; criminality in the family (brothers, sisters, parents); low intelligence or low school attainment; poor child discipline or supervision; child risk-taking and impulsivity; and family economic deprivation. However, the limitations of these theories – perhaps lacking the appropriate data and analysis – are that they fail to take period effects into account.

Traditionally, generational arguments have come to be associated with a more conservative approach to politics. In contrast, an appeal to year or period effects, particularly related to social deprivation, has traditionally been associated with the left or a more reformist approach to crime. To resolve these arguments, one needs more sophisticated data and analysis than has been used hitherto that include separating out the possible effects of age, cohort and period.

Analysing age–period–cohort effects

Our own efforts in trying to demonstrate age–period–cohort effects have focused on criminal conviction data in England and Wales (Francis et al., 2004) taken from the Home Office Offenders Index. We have taken conviction histories for six distinct birth cohorts of offenders – those born in four specific weeks in 1953, 1958, 1963, 1968, 1973 and 1978.[1] Treating males and females separately, we then examined the number of convictions for each year of age for each cohort, using the population estimates of the cohort to produce conviction rates for each age. Using conviction data rather than recorded crime data has its own problems, as we are looking only at those offenders who are dealt with and found guilty by the criminal justice system. Thus records of convictions are socially constructed in a similar way to recorded crime figures. While this should be borne in mind in the interpretation of the results of any analysis, what effects did we identify in our analysis of conviction data? Was it possible to examine whether changing conviction rates were related to age effects, period effects or cohort effects?

Before carrying out a statistical analysis, we first look at the data. A picture of these changing conviction rates for males is shown in Figure 7.2. We can see that there have been considerable changes in the patterns of offending over time. We first identify a noticeable effect for young offenders. Conviction rates for the last two birth cohorts are substantially lower for the two most recent cohorts (1973 and 1978) at young ages compared to the other four cohorts. At age 15, for example, the conviction rates for the 1973 and 1978 cohorts are about 20 convictions for every 1,000 males in the cohort, compared to a rate of between 30 and 40 convictions per thousand for those born earlier.

So what might this mean? One possibility is that the effect of a more widespread use of cautions has lowered the number of convictions per 1,000 population for the later cohorts. Whether this also reflects a lower crime rate is, of course, a moot point, for conviction rates are not necessarily a good proxy for crime rates. Nevertheless, one effect of the policy of a greater use in recent decades of cautioning does suggest that many youngsters are now being kept out of the courts – some commentators, of course, will argue that some young offenders are losing the deterrent effect of a conviction early in life (and thus one would expect a rise in the ages of those convicted in later cohorts), while others may argue that some are avoiding the deleterious effects of being labelled a criminal early in life with a court conviction (and thus one would expect a fall in the ages of those convicted in later cohorts). The effect of a policy of more widespread cautioning may both postpone the conviction of some and 'save' others from a criminal career. The story is certainly complicated but Figure 7.2 shows that following up multiple cohorts in longitudinal research in ways prescribed by Farrington (1986b) is beneficial.

Returning to the graph, we can also identify other effects. We see that there are differences between cohorts at the peak age of offending, with the 1963 birth cohort having the highest rate. There is also some evidence of the most recent birth cohorts having higher rates at later ages.

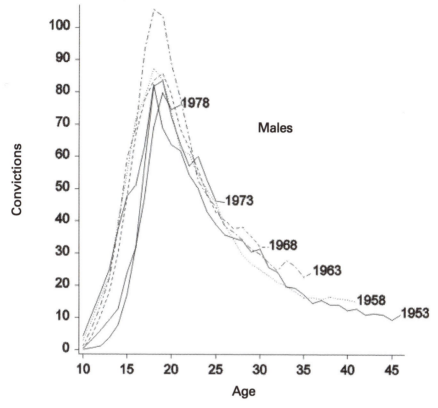

Figure 7.2 Number of convictions per 1,000 population for six male birth cohorts in England and Wales.

We can now fit a statistical model fully discussed elsewhere (Francis et al., 2004) that identifies the competing effects of age, period and cohort, while allowing for the changing cautioning policy through an age by period interaction. Such a model is complex, but we can come to some conclusions. We can identify that age effects are the most important determinant of conviction rates for both males and females. We can also identify that period effects and 'age–period interactions' are the next most important factors for both males and females. However, we also identified small but significant cohort effects, which were stronger for males than for females.

Additional work using the same data has concentrated on specific offences including burglary. We looked at the age profiles of those recruited into crime through burglary – that is, those whose first convicted offence is burglary (Soothill et al., 2004b). Labelling theorists (e.g. Becker, 1963) have stressed the importance of the first conviction in court as a significant change in an individual's public identity. In other words, being described as a 'murderer', 'thief', etc. at this stage may have different implications for the development of a deviant identity. Through a graphical analysis, we identified that for burglars, there appeared to be no strong cohort or year effects, but a strong age effect, with most 'burglary recruits' being recruited at young ages – under 20.

We contend that our results, set out more fully elsewhere (Francis et al., 2004; Soothill et al., 2004b) demonstrate that the consideration of age, period, cohort as well as gender effects is vital, and that these may well be very different for different offences. However, in terms of the practical implications of this kind of analysis, we are making limited claims. We maintain that such analysis provides with more rigour some evidence of what has actually been happening. It reinforces the view that there have been some substantial changes in the conviction rates, and provides evidence of the type of 'drivers' that may initiate change.

Conclusion

Criminologists are currently not attempting in any meaningful way to understand social change, and until social changes are incorporated into criminological thought, explanation is limited. The issues of age, period and cohort effects focus on possibilities of change over time. Thinking about changes over time is central to an applied social science study but, sadly, such thinking has been neglected, making criminological analysis appear rather static when, in fact, it must be dynamic and accommodate change. The sources of the change may be various but change there certainly is.

The three effects of age, period and cohort are something that contemporary criminologists need to understand. This is, in fact, one key purpose of this chapter – to highlight the issue of age, cohort and period effects, to stress their importance and to indicate ways to meet the methodological challenge. Two case studies have been used to demonstrate both the *need* for careful analysis and *how* to examine in detail studies addressing change in crime behaviour. When approached this way, it is clear that criminal behaviour is more complex than polemical statements seem to suggest. Debates, such as the one initiated by the Civitas work, tend to polarise the issue, where the more pertinent question to ask is the contribution of various effects of age, period and cohort. The econometric modelling case study illustrates how all statistics are not the same, even when sharing common techniques. As criminologists, we need to be able to look beyond the model, to examine its definitions and its oversights, and to provide a more robust version of 'social change'.

Of course, all studies of change in crime behaviour depend on reliable data. Data sources are available for conviction data through the Offenders Index cohort data sets. The cohorts are only collected for one in every five birth years from 1953, and this presents additional analytical problems. It is hoped that additional data will become available through self-reported offending studies and surveys such as the British Crime Survey to allow both victimisation and offending to be looked at through such methodologies. The prospects are both daunting and challenging for incorporating exploration of changes in crime patterns more routinely into criminological research.

Note

1   The Offenders Index is a court-based database of all 'standard list' criminal convictions in England and Wales from 1963 to the present day. Standard list convictions include all serious offences (triable at crown court) and many of the less serious offences which are triable at magistrates' courts only or in either court system. Criminal convictions are recorded for all offenders aged 10 or over, which is the age of criminal responsibility in England and Wales.

Chapter 8

Everyday surveillance: personal data and social classifications

David Lyon

Introduction

This chapter is about the changing nature of surveillance. Surveillance is no longer merely a matter of deliberate, individual scrutiny and consequent fears for personal privacy. It is an everyday experience, run by myriad agencies for multiple purposes and exempting no one. Interestingly, surveillance is also an ambiguous process, the two faces of which must be seen in relation to each other. So what is happening? Numerous data – including now biometric, genetic and video data – are abstracted from embodied persons and manipulated to create profiles and risk categories in a networked, rhizomic system. The resulting classifications are intended to influence and to manage populations and persons. The choices and the chances of data-subjects are thus both directly and indirectly affected, but socio-technical surveillance systems are also affected by people complying with, negotiating or resisting surveillance.

Setting the scene

In a now classic article, Malcolm Feeley and Jonathan Simon alerted their readers to the rise of 'actuarial justice', which sees crime in terms of risks and downgrades punishment in favour of regulating certain groups as 'part of a strategy of managing danger' (Feeley and Simon, 1994: 173). Since then, many others have noted from various perspectives this shift (e.g. Rose, 1999; Garland, 2001) and have also commented on the role of surveillance within it. The broad canvas is helpful for seeing the details of what I call 'everyday surveillance'. For the huge growth in surveillance techniques in the past two decades springs not merely from some technological innovations (though these are significant) but from an emerging outlook on the social world which gives a fresh dynamic to surveillance as a means of achieving certain ends.

Surveillance techniques are adopted to try to detect certain kinds of behaviours and activities in order to prevent or deter some of them. Closed circuit TV cameras may be located in stations and public transit vehicles to try to stop vandalism or violence for example. But beyond this, part of the plan may be to influence and shape the behaviour of groups or individuals to enable some kinds of activity or to close off other options. In this context, the idea of 'crime management' makes sense. Surveillance in the consumer context, for instance, may use profiles constructed from transaction trails of customer preferences and purchases to target people with highly specific advertising and incentives to buy products and services. Daily life in the global north is now monitored in myriad ways, such that we all have to pass through a series of audio, visual and data protocols in order to walk the streets, enter buildings, buy groceries, travel in road vehicles, fly from airports, surf the Internet or make telephone calls.

Surveillance in law enforcement contexts is thus just one species of the general surveillance that has mushroomed in every sphere of life in the past thirty years. But the methods used in one context may well also operate in another. It is interesting that, after the terrorist attacks of September 11, 2001, in New York (known as 9/11) members of the public in many countries are willing to countenance having their fingerprints taken for security purposes, not only for airline travel, but even for workplace security systems. Not so long ago this method carried the 'stigma' of criminality which meant that widespread resistance existed to its more general use. Viewed the other way, surveillance methods used in domains that are far from law enforcement may be introduced in an effort to reduce crime. The use of 'Customer Relationship Management' techniques by the US Department of Homeland Security since 9/11 is a case in point. If you can create profiles of potential customers by combining personal data from diverse sources and sorting them by category, similar strategies should work, it is argued, for isolating groups – especially air travellers — with the potential for violent or disruptive behaviour.

In this chapter, some examples are taken from crime and law-enforcement contexts, but others come from a wide range of activities which may have no obvious connection with crime control. Surveillance itself is discussed as a modern phenomenon that requires explanation, and its connections with 'privacy' are spelled out. I shall ask why it matters that surveillance has become so central to social processes, and what can be done about surveillance when it is seen negatively as crossing certain thresholds or becoming counterproductive. But the main focus is on how surveillance has become a means of classifying and assessing social groups so that different groups receive different treatment and the role of apparently trivial personal data in this process. In both crime control and other contexts, personal data have become centrally important to people's life chances and choices. This has both ethical and political implications that have yet to be fully understood and acted upon.

Surveillance by electronic means is an increasingly significant mode of governance in so-called knowledge-based or information societies. As Nikolas Rose nicely puts it, 'surveillance is "designed in" to the flows of everyday life' (Rose, 1999: 234). Daily routines are now subject to myriad forms of checking, watching, recording and analysing, so much so that we often take for granted the fact that we leave trails and traces wherever we are and whatever we do (Staples, 2000). But those trails and traces, however justified, are not innocent. Taken together, they are located within a network of relationships that service us, situate us and also help to organise and order our social lives. Surveillance contributes increasingly to the reproduction and reinforcing of social divisions.

Surveillance in this context means a focused attention to personal details aimed at exerting an influence over or managing the objects of the data, or 'data subjects' as they are sometimes called. Although the word surveillance often has connotations of threat, it involves inherently ambiguous processes that should not be considered in a merely negative light. Much everyday convenience, efficiency and security depends upon surveillance. Moreover, it occurs in a world where other kinds of 'mediated visibility' (Thompson, 1995: chapter 4) – particularly through television, but also using webcams and so on – are available and have a variety of effects. Surveillance is just one aspect of this mediated world. It also exhibits both hard and soft faces, which need to be distinguished. Nonetheless, surveillance does also raise questions about power, citizenship and technological development, and about information policy, regulation and resistance.

In what follows, I offer a straightforward and simple argument about everyday surveillance but one that is at odds in some significant respects with other treatments of the same themes. I argue, for example, that the rise of routinised, systematic surveillance has rather mundane origins that should not in the first place be construed as socially sinister. Surveillance is seen here as a response to the 'disappearing body' from integrative social relationships, enabled by modern means of communication and information-handling. The outcomes of this process, however, are not inconsequential as far as social order and social control are concerned. The rise of invisible information infrastructures that facilitate the classification and processing of personal data and the increasing porousness of their storage containers generate distinctive questions about everyday surveillance. These questions invite critical responses, ones that go well beyond the conventional discourses of privacy that are so often trotted out as counterpoints to surveillance.

How did surveillance become so central?

For most of human history most social interaction has been face-to-face. I say 'has been' rather than 'was' to emphasise the point that face-to-face interaction continues to be significant. But communication that takes place with the other person or persons present, in certain locales, has been supplemented by many forms of communication that do not involve co-presence and that are stretched over space. It is a key feature of modernity that using new media of communication people can interact and even remain in relationships that are integrated with others despite being divided by distance.

Fresh forms of interaction have developed as a result of this stretching of relations over space and, in some ways, over time. The new technologies are implicated in those new relationships, just because they are the means that enable them. The forms of relationship are not caused by the new technologies (which often have different uses and effects from those intended by their producers and their proponents) but the new technologies mediate them. It is striking, for example, that neither the telephone nor the Internet were conceived as means of helping ordinary people to chat with each other but that is just how they have come to be used (Marvin, 1988; Slevin, 2000). Some forms of mediated interaction have emerged over the past two centuries that are much less obviously reciprocal than phone calls or e-mail conversations. One thinks of the so-called mass media, where messages may be largely one-way, but where people are nonetheless linked in communication and symbolic exchange. Today, of course, phone-in shows on the radio and e-mail responses to television shows or newspaper articles increase the dialogical possibilities of these media.

I mention this variety of new kinds of mediated relationships to indicate that surveillance is just one among many forms of communication that have emerged as face-to-face relations of co-presence have been supplemented by so many others (Lyon, 1997). So what is special about surveillance? I suggest that as new technologies enabled more and more to be done at a distance, some compensations are sought for the fading face, the disappearing body. In earlier times, suitable compensations included a signature or a seal on a letter to authenticate its personal origin. But in the increasingly complex social settings of modernity, other tokens of trust were sought to make up for the lack of visual body clues and cues such as handshakes, eye contact and so on. Of course, the tokens of trust were sought by powerful institutions as well as in more informal contexts, which is why a critical analysis is called for.

By the twentieth century, not only the passport (Torpey, 2000) or national identification papers, but other forms of documentary evidence were required for administrative and commercial purposes. For identification at school, at the workplace or by the police, for admission to certain sites, to obtain cash from a bank or to pay for purchases, tokens of trust, of worthiness, of authentication, were required. Today our wallets and purses are stuffed with credit cards, membership numbers, phonecards, social insurance cards, driver's licences, library cards, health cards and loyalty club cards that can either be used when no other body is present for the transaction – say, at a bank machine – or when the other party is a complete stranger who needs some kind of validation for the exchange to take place.

The body has steadily disappeared from these relations but communication continues, at a distance, mediated overwhelmingly today by electronic means. From the point of view of the organisation or agency that issues the magnetic strip, the barcode or the PIN, of course, the process of checking for inclusion or of verifying identity is a means of classifying and categorising data subjects. What of the view the other way? Personal data may be released – wittingly or unwittingly – by those to whom they refer and communicated to others (the bank, the welfare department, the airline) who have some interest in them. These data are likely to be the basis of communication with the data subjects as well but beyond this the data are frequently combined in new ways and communicated between machines much more than with data subjects. What happens to those data as they are processed is largely unknown by data subjects, although some of it may be guessed when the road-toll invoice, personalised advertising or spam (electronic junk mail) appears in the mailbox or on the screen.

Paradoxes abound. Privacy, which so often is felt to be endangered by these developments, can equally be considered as a key generator of surveillance. As the more anonymous arrangements of the modern 'society of strangers' emerged and privacy was more valued, so the reciprocal need for tokens of trust grew as a means of maintaining the integrity of relations between those strangers (Nock, 1993). As the locally known, embodied person slid from view in the web of social relations, so the importance of credentials, identification and other documentary evidence was amplified. The other paradox, as I have hinted, is that the same process displays quite different faces. The means of keeping trust between strangers are at the same time the means of keeping track of the details of daily life. Privacy produces surveillance which, it is said, threatens privacy.

But not only privacy. As surveillance became a central, constitutive component of modernity, so it became increasingly a social ordering device on a steadily greater scale. This happened as more and more bureaucratic organisations undertook surveillance activities in order to maximise their efficiency and their efficacy. Keeping track is a crucial means of ensuring organisational efficiency, as Max Weber classically demonstrated (Dandeker, 1990). But keeping track requires more and more sophisticated means of classification and categorisation that both feed on surveillance data and stimulate the organisational appetite for them. Mundane means such as form-filling show how this process works, because as Brown and Duguid say, 'Forms are the crucial means by which an organization brings the heterogeneous world into line with its processes' (2000: 108). For all their apparent exactness, many gap-closing improvisations occur to make social realities fit the process, especially in residual categories of 'other'. Even in police work, where one might hope for some tight definitions, rather elastic categories such as 'annoying behaviour' may be used in creating formulaic profiles of city 'hot-spots' in cities like Toronto (Verma, 1999).

Surveillance depends, then, on information infrastructures, invisible frameworks that order the data according to certain criteria, purposes and interests. In the later twentieth century, information infrastructures were decisively computerised, which simultaneously made them even less visible and even more powerful, and also produced some specific kinds of coding (Lessig, 1999). And the kinds of interests behind social classifications expanded to include not only government departments and policing or security services, but a multitude of commercial organisations as well (Gandy, 1993; Lyon, 1994). Beyond this, particular kinds of agencies have become prominent – above all insurance companies – and their interests often transcend those of either governmental or commercial domains. They have, albeit as an unintended consequence of their activities, become very powerful social actors on the contemporary landscape (Strange, 1996).

To take just one example, there is plenty of evidence that insurance companies contribute strongly to police work in Canada. As Richard V. Ericson and Kevin D. Haggerty (1997) show, the 'risk logics' and classification schemes of external institutions such as insurance companies profoundly influence the police, who become in effect knowledge workers for them. Insurance demands lead to a shift from territories to classes of populations with varying risk levels. Biographical data are sought on populations in order to profile them in terms of probabilities and possibilities, which makes surveillance more and more systematic. Computerisation simply extends the whole process such that, in the end, they claim that 'Coercive control gives way to contingent categorization. Knowledge of risk is more important than moral culpability and punishment. Innocence declines, and everyone is assumed to be "guilty" until the risk communication system reveals otherwise …' (Ericson and Haggerty, 1997: 449).

But it is not merely that information infrastructures have significant connections with the rise of risk management and insurance classifications. Information infrastructures also enable the expansion of surveillance capacities (Rule, 1973) in several important respects. The first is that they allow for plug-ins from other sorts of technological devices, and the second, which I comment on in a moment, is that they permit greater porousness between containers. Two of the plug-ins that I have in mind are video and closed circuit television (CCTV) surveillance on the one hand, and biometrics and genetic surveillance on the other. The one has to do with the visibility of body behaviours, including in some cases the recognition of body identities, and the other with personal identification using unique body parts and the prediction of behaviours and conditions from reading genetic sequences.

It is important to note that these plug-ins depend upon the information infrastructure for their heightened surveillance capacities. For while in their own right each may contribute in specific ways to the augmenting of surveillance – by adding layers of visibility or by producing more precise identifications or predictions – it is their dependence on computer-based information infrastructures that give them their peculiar power. Without the assistance of complex and sophisticated data processing power these new technologies would remain relatively weak as means of surveillance. From the point of view of policy this is a telling development because at present the level of unquestioning acceptance of information and communication technologies is far higher than that of ethical and political critique and assessment.

The second way that information infrastructures tend to bolster surveillance capacities is that they enable networked communication between different databases. Whereas once it was fairly safe to assume that personal records kept for purposes such as health, policing, social insurance, banking and driver licensing would be stored in relatively watertight containers, the computerisation of these records means that they are readily amenable to different forms of integration. Given the immense value placed on personal data, both for commercial exploitation and for risk management, huge pressure is placed on these containers to yield their secrets in shareable ways.

Similar methods of data matching or record linkage occur in all sectors, which makes cross-tabulation technically easier. Government departments seek ways of assisting each other in obtaining compliance, but commercial organisations also exchange and trade categorised personal data in an effort to market their wares more effectively. Sometimes similar processes occur in the same place, for very different purposes. At airports, for instance, frequent flyer data, entered as passengers pass through check-in, may be used for other purposes such as car rental advertising. But personal data on airline passengers may also be exchanged for security purposes, particularly after the terrorist attacks of September 11, 2001. American and Canadian border authorities now share such data and the process is likely to escalate in other contexts as well (Whittington and Harper, 2001; Lyon, 2003).

A related issue of what might be called 'floating data' is that as some dot.com firms have failed, their databases of personal records are among the assets that can be sold off to pay creditors. So, for instance, when in 2000 a defunct company called ToySmart.com tried to sell its personal data they were challenged and obliged to sell only the entire website, and only to a related company (Stellin, 2000). Other cases may not come to light, or may be less clear cut. Again, there are both technical and legal limits to this in most jurisdictions (Flaherty, 1989; Bennett, 1992) but this does not mean that the leaky containers will suddenly stop data seeping from one to the other.

One of the key characteristics of what Manuel Castells calls the 'network society' is precisely that it is a 'space of flows' (Castells, 1996: 412). Along with the nodes and hubs in the system, dominant groups determine how and in what interests the material infrastructure operates. Among the sequences of exchange and interaction that form the flows are surveillance data, risk communication and personal information, and they, no less than any other flows, circulate according to logics embedded in asymmetries of organisational power. Concrete examples of this are offered by Clive Norris and Gary Armstrong (1999: 8) in discussing CCTV. Soccer stadia are under the camera's eye to check for (likely signs of) disorder, workplaces are watched to ensure compliance with health and safety regulations, and city centres are monitored to create and maintain ideal conditions for consumption. Differing dominant groups ensure the dispersal of discipline and its undulating, shifting quality as different sectional interests each play their part.

One outcome of this which should not be overlooked is that so-called information societies are thus by their very constitution also surveillance societies. Surveillance societies are not an accidental or malevolent result of perverse developments within information societies. Information societies – or, perhaps better, network societies (Castells, 1998) – in which advanced electronics-based information infrastructures are a central means of coordination and exchange, operate by means, among other things, of advanced surveillance operations. But they are not necessarily *maximum* surveillance societies, the possibility of which George Orwell worried about and James Rule analysed sociologically back in the 1970s. While totalitarian potential is always present, particularly in regimes that already exhibit such tendencies, the more subtle development of surveillance power is more likely.

As understood here, surveillance societies are not characterised by a single all-embracing and all-penetrating system, which is what Orwell feared above all. As Norris and Armstrong say of camera surveillance, 'CCTV has been implemented not as one pervasive system but as a series of discrete, localised systems run by a myriad of different organizations rather than a single state monolith' (Norris and Armstrong, 1999: 7). The fact that there is no single all-embracing system is no call for complacency, however. The system – or, perhaps better, 'assemblage' (Haggerty and Ericson, 2000) – expands and mutates constantly. It is augmented not only within hierarchical organisations of the sort that depict Big Brother overseeing all from the apex or the Panopticon inspector gazing out from the tower, but, more frequently, within networks that spread horizontally, reaching out here, contracting there, but always finding more ways of seeking and processing personal data with a view to management and influence.

Why does surveillance matter?

Earlier I proposed that surveillance has become a significant means of governance and of the reinforcing of social difference, and that is why the issues are important. I do not wish to downplay the fears of those who may feel that their privacy may be impugned or invaded by new kinds of surveillance technologies. They are real fears and deserve to be addressed. But to consider only personal fears about privacy distracts us from the public issues surrounding surveillance (Regan, 1995). By suggesting that surveillance has become a means of governance I mean that it serves to organise social relationships and contributes to patterns of social ordering. It does so largely through what Michel Foucault called biopower, making people up by classifying them according to categories. In the world of surveillance, such categories relate both to risk and to opportunity. Either way, what is statistically or organisationally normal becomes the touch-stone of what is right or at least appropriate (Hacking, 1990).

Categorising is an ancient process but became crucial to the rationalised social organisation of modernity. Through social convention and custom people accept their place within the hierarchy or learn to see themselves in relation to the status of others. What happens when traditional lines of authority and relationship are dismantled, to be replaced by bureaucratic rules and organisational practices? These too, are eventually accepted, even though they may now be seen as much more mutable. Who says so? Is the query heard in the democratising situations of the twentieth century, from parliament to labour union to high school? But such queries were arguably much more common in situations where face-to-face interaction still predominated. As the body disappears from integrative social relationships and is replaced by abstract tokens, so the categories too become more abstract and actuarial, and thus apparently benign. When information scientists design, delegate and choose classification systems they seldom see them as 'embodying moral and aesthetic choices that in turn craft people's identities, aspirations, and dignity' (Bowker and Star, 1999: 4). But as Lucy Suchman pithily notes, 'categories have politics' (1994).

The massive systems of computer-assisted classification that have been developed over the past thirty years are the taken-for-granted infrastructure of informational societies. They represent a concatenation of standards, practices and codes that are more or less interconnected, such that – in the case of the surveillance classifications considered here – personal and population data flows constantly through the nodes and hubs of the network. Though obvious asymmetries of power exist, no one person or body is in charge of surveillance systems; no one person or body can change them. Yet they help to make us up, to naturalise us to the institutions and agencies that invent and elaborate the categories. And they help to create the sense of who and what is rightly included and excluded, who is this, that or other (Bourdieu, 1984: 470–8). Of course, it is an empirical question as to how far and under what conditions people accept as their own the categories in which they are placed by contemporary surveillance systems (Jenkins, 2000). This is a reflexive process. But the history of medical, moral, criminal and consumer categorisation suggests that plenty of people accept such labels and live likewise.

Let me make this clear. I am not suggesting that classification and surveillance are socially negative processes. They are necessary aspects of all social situations and serve social purposes, from the vital to the vicious. The point is that as powerful means of governance, of social ordering, they are also increasingly invisible and easily taken for granted. The risk management (and other) classifications of surveillance societies involve categories that are inherently political, that call for ethical inspection. I am not suggesting either that such classifications are each powerful in the same way. Surveillance as understood here exists on a long continuum along which data is collected and processed for a range of purposes from policing and security to consumption and entertainment. It produces categorical suspicion at one end (such as ethnic profiling at airport security checks) and categorical seduction (such as targeting of potential car rental customers from lists of airline loyalty club members) at the other. Cities are increasingly splintered into socio-economically divided consumption and security enclaves by these practices (Graham and Marvin, 2001). But either way, the categories have ethics, the codes have politics.

This, then, is why surveillance matters. It does indeed provoke privacy concerns from time to time. But as expressed these personal concerns are frequently temporary and contingent ones, often relating to mistakes and errors in databases or telecommunications systems, or to loss of access to the tokens of trust such as credit cards or drivers' licences. They are not high on any political agenda. And when, for example, surveyed Internet users claim to care about online privacy, it turns out, paradoxically, that the very same persons key in PINs and credit card numbers online (*Washington Post*, 2000)! They want the benefits of e-commerce even if they also want assurances that their personal details are secure and not being used for purposes beyond the immediate transaction. When it comes to legal restrictions on surveillance, whether construed as data protection or as privacy laws, it is usually the data subject who has to make an appeal. The law only acts as a guarantee of some right to self-protection. This is why legal limits, though not insignificant, scarcely scratch the surface of the social issues raised by rapidly rising surveillance levels in everyday life.

Take the matter of voting in elections, for example. Over recent decades, the influence of television on the electoral process has frequently been noted. The whole public discourse of politics has been shaped by the perceived need for politicians to become sound byte 'personalities' in an attempt to influence the electorate. But the success of systems such as database marketing has spurred new ways of obtaining support, not least through profiling of individuals likely to give donations. The American consulting firm Aristotle International uses public sources such as motor vehicle registrations, the Postal Service and Census Bureau to obtain data on a person's age, sex, telephone number, estimated income, ethnicity, home ownership and party affiliation. It also records makes and models of cars owned, employer and occupation, whether or not they are campaign donors and how often they vote (*New York Times*, 2000). These data are manipulated to extract individual profiles of likely targets.

The above example makes no explicit use of the Internet (though it is not inconceivable that it might wish to), and refers only to personal data that are already publicly available. Moreover, activities such as this in

Canada would not be touched by existing legislation (except possibly in Quebec), and it is not clear either that they would be covered by the Personal Information Protection and Electronic Documents Act that began to come into force on 1 January 2001. While some persons may wish to object that their voting activities are private – and, after all, modern democracies have as a cardinal doctrine the idea of the secret ballot – it is also the case that persons are thus classified and categorised for particular purposes with which they may not agree. Granting or denying consent does not at present enter into data-gathering equations such as this, even though the consequences – for the dissemination of political information and for balanced awareness of alternative policies – may be far reaching. Privacy is one issue, discrimination is another (Gandy, 1995).

What can be done about surveillance?

It would make sense if some social practices and technological systems that affect everyone were also understood and actively negotiated by everyone. Such is not the case. All too often, convenience and efficiency are all that get noticed in systems that have surveillance aspects, with the result that data subjects are often unaware of the broader discriminatory and classificatory dimensions of such systems. Data protection and privacy policy and legislation have made significant strides in recent decades, even though in some cases they may be minimalist and even cynical. Data protection and privacy remain vital concerns, even if their impact on the negative aspects of social categorisation does not yet amount to much. On the other hand, what I refer to as minimalism would be seen in rules that allow only for a right of self-protection, and cynicism may be evident in cases where laws have been enacted in order to facilitate business with a trading partner rather than out of actual concern with the effects on the lives and prospects of data subjects.

At the same time, surveillance does not simply go on behind people's backs. We participate in and actively – though not always consciously – trigger the data-capture by making telephone calls, using credit cards, passing our hands over entry scanners, claiming benefits, walking down the camera-watched street, surfing the Net, and so on. Not enough is known about how people in everyday life comply with, negotiate and resist surveillance. But it is clear that workers are cautious if not negative about some electronic devices such as video, audio and computer-use monitoring, not to mention the use of biometric and genetic checks and screens. People using public spaces such as streets and private ones such as shopping malls are aware of and avoid or play up to closed circuit television systems and video surveillance. Users of Web-based e-mail accounts and online shoppers are often wary of divulging personal data when requested to do so, especially when those data seem to have little to do with the immediate transaction in question. They are aware that some other data image of them circulates in cyberspace and may well accept this as the price paid for some benefit or reward.

But it is not enough to assume that over time people will somehow 'get wise to' mushrooming surveillance systems. Such systems are a largely uninspected and unregulated means of social classification, of social ordering. They affect people's chances and their choices, and as such demand to be recognised. Beyond this, their growth calls for ethical scrutiny and democratic involvement. Of course there is an ambiguity to all such systems. Of course surveillance exhibits more than one face. But the face that is publicised is that of the smoothly running organisation, the rapid response to consumer demands or to security calls, the flexibility of the management structure, and not the negative and possibly undesirable aspects of personal data processing. The discriminatory power of con-temporary surveillance is wielded by large organisations that have strong interests in valuable personal data. The persons from whom such data are abstracted face a built-in disadvantage in this respect.

Various kinds of responses to surveillance have emerged over the past two or three decades. They may be thought of as regulative and mobilising responses (Lyon, 2001a: Chapter 8). The first is seen most obviously in the various data protection and privacy laws that now exist in most countries dependent on information infrastructures. But it is also evident in a number of voluntary, market and technical remedies for what is most usually construed as threats to privacy. Voluntary measures include company-based adherence to fair information principles. Most banks and many website operators proactively offer details of their 'privacy policies' today. Market solutions include the growing idea of making personal data earn the equivalent of royalties, such that the data subject has a tangible return for the use of his or her abstracted data. Technical solutions are various and often relate to security. The most publicised example is that of the electronic signature.

'Fair Information Principles' (that require those collecting data to use them only for the purposes stated and not for others, to obtain only that which is needed for their immediate purposes and to ensure that the data has been obtained with the knowledge and consent of the data subject, and so on) to which most privacy legislation makes reference, do not address directly the issue of the categorisation carried out by surveillance systems. They depend, implicitly but importantly, on the idea that data subjects may have an interest in controlling the flow of personal information about them. This relates to an ethically appropriate desire to disclose oneself to others only in a voluntary and limited way, and within relations of trust. And it must be said that such fair information practices, when installed, may well mitigate some negative effects of discriminatory categorisation.

But fair information practices have no brief for ethically inspecting the categories in question, still less for examining how the combined force of multiple categorisations may have the effect of strictly restricting some people's life-chances and choices while at the same time opening doors of opportunity to others. This calls for an approach that goes beyond both liberal pleas for privacy and Marxist arguments about new forms of domination in informational capitalism. Although the first leads, at best, to legal protections, these often reduce to personal property rights over personal data. As for the second, while it rightly highlights asymmetries of informational power, it can easily downplay the role of technological mediations and the role of the subject. An ethical approach, one that calls for democratic scrutiny of information systems, raises crucial issues of accountability and proposes forms of immanent critique – from within informational culture (Lyon, 2001b).

Mobilising responses, on the other hand, have grown in number and volume since the 1980s. Non-government groups and consumer movements have attempted to get to grips with the realities of the rhizomic expansion of surveillance. They may take the form of organised protest or watchdog groups – such as Privacy International or the Electronic Privacy Information Center – or ad hoc responses to specific issues. Thus attempts to create an electronic 'Australia Card' for all citizens in the mid-1980s spawned a social movement that successfully turned down the proposal, as did similar, later attempts in South Korea. Campaigns have also been mounted against specific firms and products such as the Lotus 'Marketplace: Households' software in 1994, or the Intel Pentium III chip with its unique identifier for all computers in 1999. The use of the Internet to mobilise resistance is an important part of the process.

These mobilising responses may point the way to new modes of negotiating and resisting negatively construed aspects of surveillance in the twenty-first century. It is the codes, both symbolic and electronically inscribed, that provide the means for surveillance power to flow. As Gilles Deleuze argues, physical barriers and constraint within places matter less today than the codes that enable and disable, admit and exclude, accredit or discredit (Deleuze, 1986). Audio-visual and digital protocols permit entry and movement in the city, rather than the old city gates that made the physical container so significant (Virilio, 1997: 383). As Alberto Melucci observes, social movements today are increasingly concerned with perceiving risks and identifying them as public issues, with a process of 'challenging codes' (Melucci, 1996). He argues that as everyday concerns about personal identification and life-chances become more obviously set against global flows of data and of power, new kinds of oppositional politics will emerge appropriate to the 'information age'.

Having said that, it remains true that processes associated with communication and information technologies are still regarded in rather a rosy light. Much hype surrounds the development of the Internet and the networked world in general. But the genuine benefits gleaned from having surveillance systems in place tend to deflect attention away from the inequities associated with many discriminatory dimensions of sur-veillance. And some technologies simply fare better than others in the public eye. Whereas biotechnology may be construed as 'tampering with the human body', information technologies seldom receive equally negative responses for their capacity either to 'tamper with the mind' or – still less – to produce subtle mechanisms of social ordering (Nelkin, 1995). It may turn out, of course, that as more biometric and genetic forms of surveillance become prevalent, broader questions will be raised about the classificatory power of today's codes.

The question, 'what can be done?' may thus be answered practically rather than abstractly. Many responses to surveillance have emerged and are emerging; as I suggested above, this is entirely appropriate given the increasing monitoring of everyday life. While the lead may in some instances be taken by legal initiatives, other responses are also called for, at many levels. The law, at best, can only help to create a culture of careful-ness about the processing of personal data; it cannot possibly speak to all issues, let alone keep up with each development in data mining, profiling, database targeting and marketing, locational tracking of vehicles or cellphones, and so on.

Conspiratorial and paranoid responses are counterproductive, not least because negative aspects of surveillance often arise as unintended con-sequences or by-products of other acceptable or unquestionable processes of risk management or marketing. They are also innapropriate to situations of networked, rhizomic surveillance, where no panoptic inspection tower and no omnipotent Big Brother exists. Rather, constant vigilance on the part of government departments, companies, advocacy and consumer groups, and ordinary users and citizens is called for, especially in light of the panic regimes consequent on the terrorist attacks of September 11, 2001. Focused ethical attention, along with serious proposals for democratic accountability and educational and awareness-raising initiatives, are needed if everyday surveillance is properly to be understood and, when necessary, confronted and challenged.

This chapter is adapted from an article by the author entitled 'Everyday Surveillance: personal data and social classifications', published in Information, Communication and Society, *5:2, 2002, pp. 242–257, and is reproduced with permission of the publishers (Taylor and Francis http://www.tandf.co.uk/ journals).*

Chapter 9

Conclusions

Moira Peelo and Keith Soothill

'As often as a study is cultivated by narrow minds, they will draw from it narrow conclusions.' John Stuart Mill (1865)

In reaching the final chapter, it should be clear that we see 'questioning' as central to academic endeavour. Adopting a questioning approach to academic criminology does not mean being cynical, nor does it mean that all information should be needlessly attacked. It means, instead, engaging in an informed, cogent and realistic evaluation of crime-related material, setting it in its proper context and not being tied up in a straitjacket of received or populist opinion. Questioning includes compiling then evaluating evidence, and it means approaching existing theory with respect, but not with deference. In these ways, questioning is a highly forensic and individualistic activity.

Setting criminological theory and data 'in its proper context' means accepting and recognising the socially constructed nature of crime. One important viewpoint underlying this book is that to develop an understanding of crime and criminology we need to understand the wider societal and sociological implications of all crime-related phenomena, and not just explore individual and psychological meanings. Law-making and law-breaking occur within and impact upon a political and societal arena, and individual motivations and actions need to be understood within that arena. We maintain that this viewpoint is fundamental to criminology. In other words, criminologists need to draw on a wide knowledge of society in order to make sense of criminological matters.

As we have seen in various chapters, criminology is also a debate about *how* we know about crime: what do we actually know and how do we know it? Different sorts of criminologists acknowledge different types of evidence as fundamental to knowledge of crime, and they do not all agree with each other about what constitutes data. Underlying each substantive area in this book is a set of assumptions – sometimes implicit, sometimes explicit – about what are appropriate research methods. Learning to understand those methods of data collection and analysis is a part of becoming better able to evaluate the meanings of crime-related data. Understanding criminology requires us to make sense of the sometimes conflicting methodological underpinnings of research design.

To question effectively, criminology students need to recognise that these various types of data and analysis inform us about different aspects of crime phenomena. Holdaway, for example, showed the need to separate data about *outcomes* from information about the *processes* that led to those outcomes – especially if we are interested in bringing about change. Presdee used interviews and observation in an exploration of arson and fire-raising, showing them as emotional, pleasurable activities. This allows us to understand better the *experience* of fire-raising for participants rather than approaching crime solely as a social order issue. Francis and Soothill showed us the potential for understanding *longitudinal* data sets in more depth, so beginning to address 'social change'. This requires a partnership of both sophisticated statistical modelling and an historical, sociological understanding of the period studied.

Once the socially constructed nature of crime is acknowledged, then one has to take the next step of recognising that societies – and their definitions of crime – are constantly changing. This is one reason why history is emphasised in this book. Measham, for example, has shown us the development of social attitudes towards different sorts of drug use; Lyon, in describing the 'surveillance society', is discussing a picture of life that would have been unrecognisable 50 or 70 years ago. Crime changes as the boundaries of acceptable and officially sanctioned behaviour change. Much of the time those boundaries are blurred. Our *responses* to long-standing public issues also change over time: hence Grover outlined developments in government policy towards poverty and youth and argued that these responses bring about unintended outcomes, which in turn impact on the situation.

Questioning information in these sorts of ways often means that populist politics and apparent 'common-sense' knowledge of crime are challenged by criminologists. Academic knowledge does offer something different from other kinds of knowledge: the important stance that distinguishes criminology from other crime debates is that of a questioning spirit of enquiry and challenge. Returning often to basic questions such as 'what is crime?' may seem to be asking the obvious but can be the start of a revealing investigation which, while complex, may ultimately offer up more convincing answers.

Our task of questioning can create confidence in the discipline and self-confidence in the rationale for your own viewpoint. This is not questioning just for the fun of raising doubt, but evaluating material to make a deeper sense of crime and criminology. We have stressed that we see criminology as developing a specific kind of discourse about crime, one that is conflictual and developmental. Conflict and contention within the discipline can be embraced and enjoyed, rather than resisted or feared. It is through the dynamism of conflict that we can find new levels of understanding of crime and criminology.

Criminology, like society and our understanding of crime, changes as new forms of knowledge are considered to be relevant to the understanding of crime and the criminal. To this end we want to return to the sub-text of our 'Introduction' where we suggested that crime is exciting but what of criminology?

The present context for criminology

In many ways criminology is in a remarkably buoyant state. By some measures it is healthier than ever. More students are taking criminology at undergraduate and postgraduate levels than ever before. By having the ability to attract students, vice-chancellors are willing to open or expand departments at a time when other disciplines are under threat. The rise in student demand is largely unexplained – for whatever reason, a momentum is triggered by so many new entrants to criminology.

Since the election of New Labour in 1997 there has also been a massive expansion of government-funded research into crime. This followed a notable lack of interest in criminological research in the early 1990s, especially during the period under the Conservatives when Michael Howard was Home Secretary.

So with student numbers increasing and government interest in research apparently lively, what problems could criminology possibly face? Rather than problems, we would argue that there are potential dangers waiting in store for what is, still, a relatively new discipline. Contained within the world of academe there are the snares of 'respectability' and of setting disciplinary boundaries too narrowly. In the more public world of politics, there is the question of criminologists' role in finding solutions to public problems.

Respectability and setting boundaries

Although criminology has a history, it is essentially a new discipline. New disciplines seek respectability, for it is thought that respectability brings respect. The search for respectability can produce blandness and a growing reluctance to confront controversies and conflicts within a discipline, for it is thought that controversies and conflicts bring bad publicity. However, we argue that controversies and conflicts are the very stuff of lively academic debate and, if a discipline cannot handle controversy, it will wither. Garber (2001) has argued that if disciplines are seen as static, then 'we will need more and more "studies" and "interdisciplines" to make them mirror the world' (p. 79). 'Mirroring the world' is vital work in an applied social science, hence one of the tasks of this book has been to encourage the notion that there are different ways of seeing a problem and that current 'truths' may be open to challenge.

Further, a new discipline will try to establish its 'patch'. What is it doing that other approaches are not managing to do? This is a contentious issue in criminology, for its special expertise is not always clear. Further, as Garber argues, this process of 'differentiation' can also help disciplines to protect themselves against 'self-doubt' (2001: 57). As Garber has suggested, 'boundary marking' is about certification (2001: 54), and it is certainly not unreasonable to try to delineate what undergraduates and postgraduates are supposed to gain by studying a subject within the constraints of a discipline. But there are dangers in doing so too exactly. Walklate (1998) succinctly presents the view that criminology is a shared area of concern rather than a known aspect of social reality:

> … it is a discipline inhabited by practitioners, policy makers and academics, all of whom share a common interest in that substantive issue but all of whom may be committed to quite different disciplinary ways of thinking about it, from psychiatry to sociology. This, then, gives criminology a multidisciplinary rather than a unidisciplinary character. (p. 2)

The contributors of this book have all shown that the task of criminology is to explore and explain crime, but the claim is that the boundaries with other disciplines are much more permeable than enthusiasts of the 'specialness' of criminology would recognise. In embracing the recognition that crime is a social construction, we not only want the boundaries of criminology to be ill-defined, but the potential contributions of other disciplines to be more fully appreciated.

Solutions in the public world of politics

Criminology is an applied subject, yet its relationship with governments, with the maintenance of social order and with direct applications (through workers in the justice system) are neither direct nor clear; and, sometimes, these relationships are typified by tension. While the connections are complex, it is not chance that the expansion of criminology courses within universities has come at the same time as governments have become more interested in research and opened up opportunities for graduates of criminology to work in crime-related fields. So, for example, the police service is becoming an occupation with an increasing graduate entry, and there are openings in youth justice work unimaginable even just ten years ago.

The Home Office is sponsoring research with amounts of money that attract the interest of universities, research institutes and private agencies. However, academics are concerned that the terms of the public debate about crime – or more colloquially 'law and order' – are structured in particular ways. The interest of the government in research needs to be applauded, but the dangers also need to be recognised for government – as it is perfectly entitled to do – is setting the agenda. The recent polemic by Richard Garside (2004), *Crime, Persistent Offenders and the Justice Gap* (published by the Crime and Society Foundation), challenging some core propositions and assumptions of current criminal policy, received widespread publicity but, perhaps understandably, a cool response from the government.

This is not a new concern for criminology. The dilemma for researchers concerning accepting government funds has led to divisions which, on occasions, sound a note of moral disapproval. Garber has argued that 'purity' can play an interesting part in the early self-definition of any new discipline. If, she argues, 'it undertakes to distinguish itself from another, "false" version of itself, that difference is always going to come back to haunt it' (p. 57). While we argue that conflict is essential to the dynamic development of criminology, we also ask: is it haunted by old dichotomies of 'pure' and 'false', 'good' and 'bad'? Are such binary opposites advancing criminology and do they need to be addressed in order to refresh the debate?

Ghostly opposites?

David Garland has famously pointed to the distinction between what he termed as 'the governmental project', on the one hand, and 'the Lombrosian project', on the other. By 'the governmental project' Garland meant 'the long series of empirical inquiries, which, since the eighteenth century, have sought to enhance the efficient and equitable administration of justice by charting the pattern of crime and monitoring the practice of police and prisons' (2002: 8). By 'the Lombrosian project' he points 'towards an ambitious ... theoretical project seeking to build a science of causes' (ibid.).

Hence there are those who have tried to explain crime, on the one hand, and there are those who have worked with government in 'seeking to use science in the service of management and control' (ibid.). However, Garland's point is that 'modern criminology grew out of the *convergence*' (pp. 7–8, emphasis added) of these two quite separate enterprises. Indeed, he stresses that 'the combination of the two projects seems essential to criminology's claim to be sufficiently useful and sufficiently scientific to merit the status of an accredited state-sponsored, academic discipline' (p. 8).

Garland's statement was instantly acknowledged as a useful summary of the situation, not just because the notion of convergence was embraced, but because such a divide was easily recognisable. Curiously, in describing convergence, Garland has underlined an existing division – for it still exists. Rather than total convergence, some who wish to theorise have continued to do so without being trammelled by the demands of empiricism, while those who want to establish 'social facts', sometimes supported by government money, could carry on without the demands of understanding the wider theoretical context of their findings.

Convergence, in Garland's thesis, was data meeting explanation: in an applied subject like criminology, one must ask questions if either explanation or data appear in public unaccompanied by each other. However, the natures and forms of research data and theory are varied and various, as befits a subject that is multidisciplinary in nature.

Hence a related but not identical situation is emerging in relation to methodological approaches. Increasingly, the divide has grown between those who espouse quantitative approaches and those who espouse qualitative approaches. Indeed, there is a curious place where 'positivism' and 'administrative' have converged with 'numerical' to form a composite picture of all that is perceived as unthinking, unreconstructed and oppressive, rather than joining together in Garland's constructive model of convergence.

It is not always clear which manifestation of positivism, in particular, is being addressed. Is it the development of the philosophy of positivism in the nineteenth century as attributed to Auguste Comte? Or the Lombrosian form, that said criminality was best measured by scientific methods and, as it developed, that criminals were both different to the rest of us and not responsible for their actions? Is it the 'logical positivism' of the 1920s Vienna Circle with its emphasis on inference, propositions and observable facts, constructed in opposition to the preceding dominance of theology and metaphysics? For positivism has its own history of development. The common strand is that of the notion of 'scientific method'.

Social scientists can be remarkably narrow in their interpretation of what constitutes 'scientific method' and, indeed, often do not allow for the possibility of development or diversity within 'science' (or, indeed, that scientists and statisticians may not be aiming to achieve the same intellectual ends as social scientists). Measurement, a part of the Lombrosian quest for 'a science of causes', is associated with statistics; statistics is associated with government research; ergo, anything numerical is positivist within a model of science, probably established in the nineteenth century.

What is seen as key here is not good or bad arithmetic, or good or bad research methods, but what one does with observed crime phenomena – whether quantitative or qualitative. As Holdaway has argued in this book, knowing the numbers of 'stop and search' is not enough to bring about change. It is interpretation and analysis that are the keys, in these examples, to determining how meaningful data can be. Interpretation and analysis do, of course, reflect the researcher's underlying philosophy. While this methodology must be evaluated, its meanings can no longer be assumed just by use of particular methods of research.

Conflict and dispute drive a discipline forward, but going over the same ground endlessly does not. If the terminology used to describe other criminologists implies moral disapproval (currently 'positivist' and 'empiricist' contain overtones of disdain and 'qualitative' and 'quantitative' are about joining up with different teams), then this is a moment to start questioning more deeply what is going on. Students of criminology are not obliged to inherit and reproduce the feuds of their forebears and must always question how useful old or existing feuds are for the criminological issues they are facing. The crime agenda and social issues facing future generations of criminologists will be different to those we consider today, and so one must always ask: do existing divisions help or hinder my understanding of crime and criminology? What do I keep that is useful from past theorising and what can I usefully build on? In posing these questions, we are putting forward the idea that criminology is not only a contested discourse, but one that is reactive and dynamic – responsive to a continual process of social change.

Change

Historians agree that the last 30 years have seen unprecedented social change in the United Kingdom. Rosen (2003), for example, has argued that key social institutions – for example, religion, the monarchy and aristocracy, trade unions and marriage – all saw a decline in popular support from the 1950s onwards, with both good and bad consequences:

> The decline in the prestige and influence of these institutions was but
> one of the long-term developments which helped to create a more
> flexible and less hidebound society in which diversity flourished at
> the expense of some of the easy certainties of yesteryear. (p. 39)

Harris (2003) has argued that many aspects of human behaviour once
viewed as deviant are now largely acceptable aspects of life, such as
illegitimacy, homosexuality and partnerships outside marriage (pp. 116–
17). Peelo has indicated (see Chapter 2) how, during this same period,
crime became not only a highly politicised issue (see Garland, 2001;
Downes and Morgan, 2002) but one with plentiful media coverage, both in
fictional drama and in news reports (see Reiner, 2002; Jewkes, 2004).

It is not surprising, then, in the light of all these changes, that
criminology itself has been changing. Soothill has argued, in this book (see
Chapter 1), that individual attempts to produce large-scale theory that
explain crime are best understood as reflections of their time. Elsewhere,
Walklate (1998) has acknowledged that there is a history (a 'backcloth' or
'common threads') to criminology, but she sees recent developments since
the 1970s as producing a criminology that is quite different to what went
before. These developments are, Walklate argues, a combination of
changes in academic theorising and changes within society. She described
what went before, in the development of both policy debate and knowledge about crime, as concerned with a 'desire to produce and work with
the objectively measurable facts of crime' (p. 130). She identifies this as
fundamentally a masculinist approach, in that it has equated 'human'
experience with male experience. Feminist thought, for Walklate then, is
one substantial area of theoretical change. Other areas with a profound
impact on the crime agenda are the role of 'risk' and the relationship of the
citizen to the state (see Chapter 8).

Taylor (1999) offers another example of both social and theoretical
change. He argues, as we do, that to understand crime criminologists must
understand its context. He offers a market explanation of this context,
explaining that society has moved from a Fordist to a post-Fordist,
competitive market that has deconstructed prior welfare systems. This
thesis allows criminologists to have a framework for explaining the social
and market context for crime which moves away from the critiques of
capitalism found in the 1960s and 1970s. Such a framework links theory to
the actuality of the current historical period.

A multidisciplinary community that shares a common interest in crime
and criminality is not one that will be in accord. People reflect different
mindsets, and they are committed to different philosophies that inform
their research questions, choice of research methods and their interpretation and analyses of data. All this, we argue, is set within an evolving

social context. There should be no expectation, then, of agreement about the goals of criminology or expectation of a global explanation of crime.

So criminology students have to keep their own 'running total' of explanations in a complex subject and continue to question criminology:

- How much does it satisfy my curiosity about crime?
- Does it help me to understand better how societies reach agreement about transgression?
- Does it help me to understand how society polices and punishes transgression?
- Do I understand better who offends and why they offend and who is caught?
- Does criminology's theorising and data analysis take me further in unravelling these crime-related phenomena?

Internecine struggles between criminologists can, if understood, throw more light on crime and criminality – but that does not mean that you, the student, have to agree exactly with existing viewpoints.

Engagement with the process of sifting through and working out which theories, which approaches and which questions remain relevant to today's problems must be matched with a detailed understanding of current social trends and concerns. Where does your theorising stand in relation to other explanations of crime and criminality?

When constructing your own framework for making sense of these issues, remember that while criminology is an intellectual endeavour it has, at its heart, a human and humane focus on a subject that touches all our lives – as victims, as offenders and as fellow members of society.

References

Abbott, P. and Wallace, C. (1992) *The Family and the New Right*. London: Pluto Press.

Abercrombie, N., Warde, A., Deem, R., Penna, S., Soothill, K., Urry, J., Sayer, A. and Walby, S. (2000) *Contemporary British Society*, 3rd edn. Cambridge: Polity Press.

Ahmad, M. and Mwenda, L. (2004) *Drug Seizure and Offender Statistics, United Kingdom, 2001 and 2002*, Home Office Statistical Bulletin 08/04. London: Home Office.

Alcock, P. (1987) *Poverty and State Support*. Harlow: Longman.

Alcock, P. (1993) *Understanding Poverty*. Basingstoke: Macmillan.

Aldridge, J., Parker, H. and Measham, F. (1999) *Drug Trying and Drug Use across Adolescence: A Longitudinal Study of Young People's Drug Taking in Two Regions of Northern England*, DPAS Paper No. 1. London: Home Office.

Altheide, D. L. and Snow, R. P. (1979) *Media Logic*. Beverly Hills, CA: Sage.

Bachelard, G. (1964) *Psychoanalysis of Fire*. London: Routledge & Kegan Paul.

Bakhtin, M. (1984) *Rabelais and his World*. Bloomington, IN: Indiana University Press.

Banton, M. (1987) *Racial Theories*. Cambridge: Cambridge University Press.

Barclay, P. (chair) (1995) *Inquiry into Income and Wealth*, Vol. 1. York: Joseph Rowntree Foundation.

Barker, M. (1981) *The New Racism*. London: Junction Books.

Barnett, S. and Gaber, I. (2001) *Westminster Tales: The Twenty-first-Century Crisis in Political Journalism*. Continuum: London.

Barnouw, V. (1979) *Anthropology: A General Introduction*. Homewood, IL: Dorsey Press.

Barth, F. (ed.) (1969) *Ethnic Groups and Boundaries: The Social Organisation of Cultural Difference*. Boston, MA: Little, Brown.

Bean, P. (2004) *Drugs and Crime*, 2nd edn. Cullompton: Willan.

Becker, H. (1963) *Outsiders: Studies in the Sociology of Deviance.* London: Free Press of Glencoe (republished 1973).

Beechey, V. and Perkins, T. (1987) *A Matter of Hours: Women, Part-Time Work and the Labour Market.* Cambridge: Polity Press.

Bennett, C. (1992) *Regulating Privacy: Data Protection and Public Policy in Europe and the United States.* Ithaca, NY: Cornell University Press.

Bennett, T. (1998) *Drugs and Crime: The Results of Research on Drug Testing and Interviewing Arrestees.* Research Study No. 183. London: Home Office Research and Statistics Directorate.

Benson, B., Sebastian Leburn, I. and Rasmussen, D. (2001) 'The impact of drug enforcement on crime: an investigation of the opportunity cost of police resources', *Journal of Drug Issues*, 31(4): 989–1006.

Benson, M. L. and Moore, E. (1992) 'Are white-collar and common offenders the same? An empirical and theoretical critique of a recently proposed general theory of crime', *Journal of Crime and Delinquency*, 29: 251–72.

Bentley, T., Oakley, K. with Gibson, S. and Kilgour, K. (1999) *The Real Deal: What Young People Really Think about Government, Politics and Social Exclusion.* London: Demos.

Berridge, V. (1980) 'The making of the Rolleston Report, 1908–1926', *Journal of Drug Issues*, 10: 7–28.

Berridge, V. (1981) *Opium and the People: Opiate Use and Drug Control Policy in Nineteenth and Early Twentieth Century England.* London: Free Association Books.

Berridge, V. (1984) 'Drugs and social policy: the establishment of drug control in Britain, 1900–30', *British Journal of Addiction*, 79: 17–29.

Best, D., Strang, J., Beswick, T. and Gossop, M. (2001) 'Assessment of a concentrated, high-profile police operation: No discernible impact on drug availability, price or purity', *British Journal of Criminology*, 41: 738–45.

Bivand, P. (2002) 'Rights and duties in the New Deal', *Working Brief*, 136: 15–17.

Black, J. (2004) *Britain Since the Seventies.* London: Reaktion Books.

Blackman, S. (2004) *Chilling Out: The Cultural Politics of Substance Consumption, Youth and Drug Policy.* Maidenhead: Open University Press, p. 227.

Blair, T. (2004) Speech on the launch of the five-year strategy for crime, at: http://www.number10.gov.uk'output/Page6129.asp (accessed 18 August 2004).

Bland, N., Miller, J. and Quinton, P. (2000) *Managing the Use and Impact of Searches: A review of force interventions.* London: Home Office.

Booth Davies, J. (1992) *The Myth of Addiction*, 2nd edn, Amsterdam: Harwood.

Bottoms, A. and Wiles, P. (2002) 'Environmental criminology', in M. Maguire, R. Morgan, and R. Reiner (eds), *The Oxford Handbook of Criminology*, 3rd edn. Oxford: Oxford University Press, pp. 620–56.

Bourdieu, P. (1984) *Distinction: A Social Critique of the Judgement of Taste.* London and New York: Routledge.

Bowker, G. and Star, S. L. (1999) *Sorting Things Out: Classification and its Consequences.* Cambridge, MA: MIT Press.

Bowling, B. and Phillips, C. (2000) *Racism, Crime and Justice.* Harlow: Pearson.

Bowling, P., Graham, J. and Ross, A. (1994) 'Self-reported offending among young people in England and Wales', in J. Junger-Tas, G. Terlouw and M. Klein (eds), *Delinquent Behaviour Among Young People in the Western World*. Amsterdam: Kugler, pp. 42–64.

Box, S. (1987) *Recession, Crime and Unemployment*. Basingstoke: Macmillan.

Brain, K. (2000) *Youth, Alcohol and the Emergence of the Post-Modern Alcohol Order*. Occasional Paper No. 1. London: Institute of Alcohol Studies.

Brain, K., Parker, H. and Bottomley, T. (1998) *Evolving Crack Cocaine Careers*. Research Findings No. 85. London: Home Office, Home Office Research, Development and Statistics Directorate.

Brewer, M., Goodman, A., Myck, M., Shaw, J. and Shephard, A. (2004) *Poverty and Inequality in Britain: 2004*, Commentary 96. London: Institute for Fiscal Studies.

Brinton, C. K. (1941) *Nietzsche*. Cambridge, MA: Harvard University Press.

Brown, J. S. and Duguid, P. (2000) *The Social Life of Information*. Boston, MA: Harvard Business School Press.

Brown, J. and Kreft, I. (1998) 'Zero effects of drug prevention programmes', *Evaluation Review*, 22: 3–4.

Burke, E. (1757) 'A Philosophical Enquiry into the Origin of our Ideas of the Sublime and Beautiful', in A. Philips (ed.) (1990) *Oxford World Classics*. Oxford: Oxford University Press.

Burrell, I. and Goodchild, S. (2002) 'Stops and searches of blacks on the rise', *Independent*, 10th March.

Calhoun, C. (2003) *Guardian*, obituary notice, 3 March.

Callinicos, A. (2001) *Against the Third Way*. Cambridge: Polity Press.

Callinicos, A. and Simons, M. (1985) *The Great Strike: The Miners' Strike of 1984–5 and Its Lessons*. London: Bookmarks Publications.

Carlen, P. (1988) *Women, Crime and Poverty*. Buckingham: Open University Press.

Carmichael, F. and Ward, R. (2000) 'Youth unemployment and crime in England and Wales', *Applied Economics*, 32: 559–71.

Castells, M. (1996) *The Rise of the Network Society*. Oxford and Malden, MA: Blackwell.

Castells, M. (1998) 'Materials for an exploratory theory of the network society', *British Journal of Sociology*, 51(1): 5–24.

Catalano, R. F. and Hawkins, J. D. (1996) 'The social development model: a theory of antisocial behavior', in J. D. Hawkins (ed.), *Delinquency and Crime: Current Theories*. Cambridge: Cambridge University Press.

Caulkins, J., Rydell, C., Everingham, F., Chiesa, J. and Bushway, S. (1999) *An Ounce of Prevention, a Pound of Uncertainty: The Cost Effectiveness of School Based Drug Prevention Programmes*. Santa Monica, CA: RAND.

Chadwick, L. and Scraton, P. (2001) 'Critical criminology', E. McLaughlin and J. Muncie (eds), *The Sage Dictionary of Criminology*. London: Sage, pp.70–2.

Chan, J. B. L. (1997) *Changing Police Culture*. Cambridge: Cambridge University Press.

Chatterton, M. R. (1992) 'Controlling Police Work. Strategies and tactics of the lower ranks – their past and future relevance.' Unpublished paper presented at conference, Social Order in Post Classical Sociology, University of Bristol.

Chibnall, S. (1977) *Law and Order News: An Analysis of Crime Reporting in the British Press*. London: Tavistock.

Chiricos, T. (1987) 'Rates of crime and unemployment: an analysis of aggregate research evidence', *Social Problems*, 34: 187–212.

Clarke, T. and Taylor, J. (1999) 'Income inequality: a tale of two cycles?', *Fiscal Studies*, 20: 387–408.

Cockerell, M. (1988) *Live From Number 10: The Insider Story of Prime Ministers and Television*. London: Faber & Faber.

Coffield, F. and Gofton, L. (1994) *Drugs and Young People*. London: Institute for Public Policy Research.

Cohen, P. (1993) *Home Rules*. London: New Ethnicities Unit, University of East London.

Cohen S. (1988) *Against Criminology*. New Brunswick, NJ: Transaction Books.

Cohen, S. (2002) *Folk Devils and Moral Panics: the Creation of Mods and Rockers*, 3rd ed. London: Routledge (originally printed 1972).

Cohen, L. and Felson, M. (1979) 'Social change and crime rate trends: a routine activities approach', *American Sociological Review*, 46: 505–24.

Coleman, C. and Moynihan, J. (1996) *Understanding Crime Data: Haunted by the Dark Figure*. Buckingham: Open University Press.

Collin, M. and Godfrey, J. (1997) *Altered State: The Story of Ecstasy Culture and Acid House*. London: Serpent's Tail.

Condon, J. and Smith, N. (2003) *Prevalence of Drug Use: Key Findings from the 2002/2003 British Crime Survey*. Home Office Research Findings No. 229. London: Home Office.

Cook, D. (1997) *Poverty, Crime and Punishment*. London: Child Poverty Action Group.

Corkery, J. (2002) *Drug Seizure and Offender Statistics, United Kingdom, 2000*. Home Office Statistical Bulletin 4/02. London: Home Office.

Cowan, R. (2004) 'Police photo campaign shows ravages of addiction', *Guardian*, 2 November.

Cronin, A. (2004) *Advertising Myths: The Strange Half-lives of Images and Commodities*. London: Routledge.

Curtis, R. (2002) 'Coexisting in the real world: the problems, surprises and delights of being an ethnographer on a multidisciplinary research project'. *International Journal of Drug Policy*, 13: 297–310.

Dandeker, C. (1990) *Surveillance, Power, and Modernity*. Cambridge: Polity Press.

Deacon, A. (1997) 'Lawrence Mead and the new politics of welfare', in L. Mead (ed.), *From Welfare to Work: Lessons from America*. London: Institute of Economic Affairs, Health and Welfare Unit, pp. xii–xvi.

Deacon, A. (2000) 'Learning from the US? The influence of American ideas upon "new labour" thinking on welfare reform', *Policy and Politics*, 28(1): 5–18.

Deacon, A. (2002) *Perspectives on Welfare*. Buckingham: Open University Press.

Deadman, D. (2003) 'Forecasting Residential Burglary', *International Journal of Forecasting*, 19: 567–78.

Deehan, A. (1999) *Alcohol and Crime: Taking Stock*. Crime Reduction Research Series Paper No. 3. London: Home Office, Policing and Reducing Crime Unit. Also available at: http://www.homeoffice.gov.uk/rds/index.htm

Deleuze, G. (1986) 'Postscript on the societies of control', *October*, 59: 3–7.

Dennis, N. and Erdos, G. (2005) *Cultures and Crimes: Policing in Four Nations*. London: Civitas.

Denscombe, M. (2001) 'Uncertain identities and health-risking behaviour: the case of young people and smoking in late modernity', *British Journal of Sociology*, 52(1): 157–77.

Department of Work and Pensions (2004) *Measuring Child Poverty*. London: Department of Work and Pensions.

Dhiri, S., Brand, S., Harries, R. and Price, R. (1999) *Modelling and Predicting Property Crime Trends*. Home Office Research Study 195. London: HMSO. Online at: http://www.homeoffice.gov.uk/rds/

Ditton, J. and Duffy, J. (1983) 'Bias in the newspaper reporting of crime news', *British Journal of Criminology*, 23(2): 159–65.

Ditton, J., Chadee, D., Farrall, S., Gilchrist, E. and Bannister, J. (2004) 'From imitation to intimidation: a note on the curious and changing relationship between the media, crime and fear of crime', *British Journal of Criminology*, 44(4): 595–610.

Dorn, N. and Jamieson, A. (2000) *Room for Manoeuvre: Overview of Comparative Legal Research into National Drug Laws of France, Germany, Italy, Spain, the Netherlands and Sweden and Their Relation to Three International Drugs Conventions*. London: DrugScope. Also available at: http://www.drugscope.org.uk

Dorn, N. and Murji, K. (1992) *Drug Prevention: A Review of the English Language Literature*, Research Monograph No. 5. London: Institute for the Study of Drug Dependence.

Downes, D. and Morgan, R. (2002) 'The skeletons in the cupboard: the politics of law and order at the turn of the Millennium', in M. Maguire, R. Morgan and R. Reiner (eds), *The Oxford Handbook of Criminology*, 3rd edn. Oxford: Oxford University Press, pp. 286–321.

Downes, D. and Rock, P. (1998) *Understanding Deviance: A Guide to the Sociology of Crime and Rule Breaking*, 3rd edn. Oxford: Oxford University Press.

Dromey, J. and Taylor, G. (1978) *Grunwick: The Workers' Story*. London: Lawrence & Wishart.

Dublin Principles of Co-operation among the Beverage Alcohol Industry, Governments, Scientific Researchers, and the Public Health Community (1997). Dublin: National College of Ireland.

Ducker, J. (2004) '24-hour licences are "vital"', *Manchester Metro News*, 24 September.

Duff, C. (2005) 'Party drugs and party people: examining the "normalization" of recreational drug use in Melbourne, Australia', *International Journal of Drug Policy*, forthcoming.

Edwards, G. (2000) *Alcohol: The World's Favourite Drug*. New York: Thomas Dunne.

Elliott, C. and Ellingworth, D. (1998) 'Exploring the relationship between unemployment and property crime', *Applied Economic Letters*, 5(8): 527–30.

Ellison, E. (2004) 'Policing cannabis: can pragmatism replace policy?', *Probation Journal*, 51(4): 415–20.

Engineer, R., Phillips, A., Thompson, J. and Nicholls, J. (2003) *Drunk and Disorderly: A Qualitative Study of Binge Drinking Among 18 to 24 Year Olds*, Home Office Research Study No. 262. London: Home Office.

Ericson, R. V. and Haggerty, K. (1997) *Policing the Risk Society*. Toronto: University of Toronto Press.

Ettorre, E. (1992) *Women and Substance Use*. Basingstoke: Macmillan.

Ettorre, E. (2004) 'Revisioning women and drug use: gender sensitivity, embodiment and reducing harm', *International Journal of Drug Policy*, Special Edition: Social Theory in Drug Research and Harm Reduction, 15(5–6).

Etzioni, A. (1995) *The Spirit of Community. Rights, Responsibilities and the Communitarian Agenda*. London: Fontana Press.

Etzioni, A. (1997) *The New Golden Rule*. London: Profile Books.

Farrington, D. (1986a) 'Stepping stones to adult criminal careers', in D. Olweus, J. Block and M. Radke-Yarrow (eds), *Development of Antisocial and Prosocial Behavior*. New York: Academic Press, pp. 359–84.

Farrington, D. (1986b) 'Age and crime', *Crime and Justice*, 7: 189–250.

Farrington, D. (1990) 'Implications of criminal career research for the prevention of offending', *Journal of Adolescence*, 13: 93–113.

Farrington, D. (1995) 'The development of offending and antisocial behaviour from childhood: key findings from the Cambridge study in delinquent development', *Journal of Child Psychology and Psychiatry*, 36: 929–64.

Farrington, D. P. (2003) 'Developmental and life-course criminology: key theoretical and empirical issues – the 2002 Sutherland Award Address', *Criminology*, 41(2): 221–55.

Farrington, D., Gallagher, B., Morley, L. and St Ledger, R. (1986) 'Unemployment, school leaving, and crime', *British Journal of Criminology*, 26: 335–56.

Feeley, M. and Simon, J. (1994) 'Actuarial justice: the emerging new criminal law', in D. Nelken (ed.), *The Futures of Criminology*. London: Sage, pp. 173–201.

Felson, M. (1998) *Crime and Everyday Life*. Thousand Oaks, CA: Pine Forge Press.

Ferrell, J. (2005) 'Cultural criminology', in *Blackwell Encyclopedia of Sociology*, ed. G. Ritzner. Oxford: Blackwell (forthcoming).

Ferrell, J., Hayward, K., Morrison, W. and Presdee, M. (2004) *Cultural Criminology Unleashed*. London: Glasshouse.

Field, S. (1990) *Trends in Crime and Their Interpretation: A Study of Recorded Crime in Post-War England and Wales,* Home Office Research Study 119. London: HMSO.

Field, S. (1999) *Trends in Crime Revisited*, Home Office Research Study 195. London: Home Office. Online at http://www.homeoffice.gov.uk/rds/.

FitzGerald, M. (1999) *Searches in London: Under s1 of the Police and Criminal Evidence Act*. London: Metropolitan Police Service.

Fitzpatrick, M. (2001) *The Tyranny of Health: Doctors and the Regulation of Lifestyle*. London: Routledge.

Flaherty, D. (1989) *Protecting Privacy in Surveillance Societies*. Chapel Hill, NC: University of North Carolina Press.

Flaherty, J., Veit-Wilson, J. and Dornan, P. (2004) *Poverty: The Facts*, 5th edn. London: Child Poverty Action Group.

Fountain, J., Bashford, J., Underwood, S., Khurana, J., Winters, M., Carpentier, C. and Patel, K. (2004) 'Drug use amongst Black and minority ethnic communities in the European Union and Norway', *Probation Journal*, 51(4): 362–78.

Foxcroft, D., Lister-Sharp, D. and Lowe, G. (1997) 'Alcohol misuse prevention for young people: a systematic review reveals methodological concerns and lack of reliable evidence of effectiveness', *Addiction*, 92(5): 531–37.

Francis, B., Soothill, K. and Ackerley, E (2004) 'Multiple cohort data, delinquent generations and criminal careers', *Journal of Contemporary Criminal Justice*, 20(2):103–26.

Frazer, J. G. (1922) *The Golden Bough*. New York: Macmillan.

Freud, S. (1955) *Civilisation and Its Discontents*. London: Hogarth.

Friedman, M. (1962) *Capitalism and Freedom*. Chicago, IL: University of Chicago Press.

Gandy, O. H. (1993) *The Panoptic Sort: A Political Economy of Personal Information*. Boulder, CO: Westview.

Gandy, O. H. (1995) 'It's discrimination, stupid!', in J. Brook and I. A. Boal (eds), *Resisting the Virtual Life: The Culture and Politics of Information*. San Francisco, CA: *City Lights*, pp. 35–48.

Garber, M. (2001) *Academic Instincts*. Princeton, NJ: Princeton University Press.

Garland, D. (2001) *The Culture of Control*. Oxford: Oxford University Press.

Garland, D. (2002) 'Of crimes and criminals: The development of criminology in Britain', in M. Maguire, R. Morgan and R. Reiner (eds), *The Oxford Handbook of Criminology*, 3rd edn. Oxford: Oxford University Press, pp. 7–50.

Garside, R. (2004) *Crime, Persistent Offenders and the Justice Gap*. London: Crime and Society Foundation.

Geneva Partnership on Alcohol: Towards a Global Charter (2000) Washington DC: International Centre for Alcohol Policies.

Gilbert, H. and Warburton, D. (2000) 'Craving: a problematic concept in smoking research', *Addiction Research*, 8(4): 381–98.

Giles, F. T. (1963) *The Criminal Law*, 3rd edn. London: Penguin Books.

Gilroy, P. (1982) 'The myth of black criminality', in M. Eve and D. Musson (eds), *Socialist Register, 1982*. London: Merlin, pp. 47–56.

Ginsburg, N. (1979) *Class, Capital and Social Policy*. London: Macmillan.

Goddard, H. H. (1914) *Feeble-Mindedness: Its Causes and Consequences*. New York: Macmillan.

Gofton, L. (1990) 'On the town: drink and the "new lawlessness"', *Youth and Society*, 29 (April): 33–9.

Goldson, B. and Jamieson, J. (2002) 'Youth crime, the "parenting deficit" and state intervention: a contextual critique', *Youth Justice*, 2(2): 82–99.

Gordon, P. and Newnham, A. (1985) *Passport to Benefits*. London: Child Poverty Action Group.

Gottfredson, M. R. and Hirschi, T. (1990) *A General Theory of Crime*. Stanford, CA: Stanford University Press.

Goudsblom, J. (1992) *Fire and Civilisation*. London: Allen Lane.

Gough, I. (1979) *The Political Economy of the Welfare State*. London: Macmillan.

Graham, H. (1989) 'Women and smoking in the United Kingdom: the implications for health promotion', *Health Promotion*, 3(4): 371–82.

Graham, H. (1994) 'Surviving by smoking', in S. Wilkinson and C. Kitzinger (eds), *Women and Health: Feminist Perspectives*. London: Taylor and Francis, pp. 102–23.

Graham, H. and Blackburn, C. (1998) 'The socio-economic patterning of health and smoking behaviour among mothers with young children on income support', *Sociology of Health and Illness*, 20(2): 215–40.

Graham, J. and Bowling, B. (1995) *Young People and Crime*, Home Office Research Study No. 145. London: Home Office.

Graham, S. and Marvin, S. (2001) *Splintering Urbanism: Networked Infrastructures, Technological Mobilities, and the Urban Condition*. London and New York: Routledge.

Greer, C. (2003) *Sex Crime and the Media: Sex Offending and the Press in a Divided Society*. Cullompton: Willan.

Grover, C. (2005) 'Living wages and the "Making Work Pay" strategy', *Critical Social Policy*, 25(1): 5–27.

Grover, C. and Stewart, J. (2002) *The Work Connection*. Basingstoke: Palgrave.

Hacking, I. (1990) *The Taming of Chance*. Cambridge, New York and Melbourne: Cambridge University Press.

Haggerty, K. and Ericson, R. V. (2000) 'The surveillant assemblage', *British Journal of Sociology*, 51(4): 605–22.

Hale, C. (1998) 'Crime and the business cycle in post-war Britain revisited', *British Journal of Criminology*, 38(4): 681–98.

Hales, J. and Collins, D. (1999) *New Deal for Young People: Leavers with Unknown Destinations*, Employment Service Research Report 21. Sheffield: Employment Service.

Hall, S. (1992) 'New ethnicities', in J. Donald and A. Rattansi (eds), *Race, Culture and Difference*. London: Sage, pp. 252–9.

Halsey, A. (1993) 'Foreword', in N. Dennis and G. Erdos (eds), *Families Without Fatherhood*. London: Institute of Economic Affairs Health and Welfare Unit, pp. ix–xiii.

Hammersley, R., Marsland, L. and Reid, M. (2003) *Substance Use by Young Offenders: The Impact of the Normalisation of Drug Use in the Early Years of the 21st Century*, Home Office Research Study No. 261. London: Home Office RDS Directorate.

Hanscombe, A. (1996) *The Last Thursday in July: The Story of Those Left Behind*. London: Century.

Harries, R. (2003) 'Modelling and predicting property crime trends in England and Wales – a retrospective', *International Journal of Forecasting*, 19: 557–66.

Harris, J. (2003) 'Tradition and transformation: society and civil society in Britain, 1945–2001', in K. Burk (ed.), *The British Isles since 1945*. Oxford: Oxford University Press, pp. 91–125.

Haslam, J. (1999) *The Vices of Integrity: E. H. Carr, 1892–1982*. London: Verso.

Hayek, F. (1960) *The Constitution of Liberty*. London: Routledge & Kegan Paul.

Hayward, K. (2004a) 'Space – the final frontier: criminology, the city and the spatial dynamics of exclusion', in J. Ferrell, K. Hayward, W. Morrison and M. Presdee (eds), *Cultural Criminology Unleashed*. London: Glasshouse, pp.155–67.

Hayward, K. (2004b) *City Limits: Crime, Consumer Culture and the Urban Experience*. London: Glasshouse.

Hellawell, K. (2002) *The Outsider: The Autobiography of One of Britain's Most Controversial Policemen*. London: HarperCollins.

Henderson, S. (1993) 'Luvdup and de-elited: responses to drug use in the second decade', in P. Aggleton, P. Davies and G. Hart (eds), *AIDS: Facing the Second Decade*. London: Falmer, pp. 119–30.

Henderson, S. (1999) 'Drugs and culture: the question of gender', in N. South (ed.), *Drugs: Cultures, Controls and Everyday Life*. London: Sage, pp. 36–48.

Her Majesty's Inspector of Constabulary (1995) *Developing Diversity in the Police Service: Equal Opportunities Thematic Inspection Report, 1995*. London: Home Office.

Her Majesty's Inspectorate of Constabulary (1992) *Equal Opportunities in the Police Service*. London: Home Office.

Her Majesty's Inspectorate of Constabulary (1996) *Developing Diversity in the Police Service*. London: Home Office.

Her Majesty's Inspectorate of Constabulary (1997) *Winning the Race: Policing Plural Communities*. London: Home Office.

Her Majesty's Inspectorate of Constabulary (1999) *Winning the Race: Policing Plural Communities Revisited*. London: Home Office.

Hilton, M., (2000) *Smoking in British Popular Culture 1800–2000: Perfect Pleasures*. Manchester: Manchester University.

Hinchliff, S. (2001) 'The meaning of ecstasy use and clubbing to women in the late 1990s', *International Journal of Drug Policy*, 12(5–6): 455–68.

Hirschi, T. (1969) *Causes of Delinquency*. Berkeley, CA: University of California Press.

Hobbs, D., Lister, S., Hadfield, P., Winlow, S. and Hall, S. (2000) 'Receiving shadows: governance and liminality in the night-time economy', *British Journal of Sociology*, 51(4): 701–18.

Hobsbawm, E. (2005) 'In defence of history', *Guardian*, 15 January.

Holdaway, S. (1983) *Inside the British Police: A Force at Work*. Oxford: Blackwell.

Holdaway, S. (1991) *Recruiting a Multi-Racial Police Force*. London: HMSO.

Holdaway, S. (1996) *The Racialisation of British Policing*. Basingstoke: Macmillan.

Holdaway, S. (1997a) 'Constructing and sustaining "race" within the police workforce', *British Journal of Sociology*, 48(1): 19–34.

Holdaway, S. (1997b) 'Some recent approaches to the study of race in criminological research: race as social process', *British Journal of Criminology*, 37(3): 383–400.

Holdaway, S. (1999) 'Understanding the police investigation of the murder of Stephen Lawrence: a "mundane sociological analysis"', *Sociological Research Online*, 4(1).

Holdaway, S., Davidson, N., Dignan, J., Hammersley, R. and Marsh, P. (2001) *New Strategies to Address Youth Offending*. London: HMSO.

Hollin, C. R. (2002) 'Criminological psychology', in M. Maguire, R. Morgan and R. Reiner (eds), *The Oxford Handbook of Criminology*, 3rd edn. Oxford: Oxford University Press, pp. 144–74.

Home Office (2000) *Statistics on Race and the Criminal Justice System: A Home Office Publication under section 95 of the Criminal Justice Act 1991*. London: Home Office.

Home Office (2002) *Crime in England and Wales, 2001–2*, HOSB 7/02 (Home Office Statistical Bulletin). London: Home Office.

Home Office (2003) *Home Secretary's Action Plan: Fourth Annual Report on Progress*. London: Home Office.

Hunt, M. (1961) 'A biographical profile of Robert K. Merton', *The New Yorker*, 28: 39–63.

Jackson, M. (1989) *Paths Towards a Clearing: Radical Empiricism and Ethnographic Inquiry*. Bloomington, IN: Indiana University Press.

Jefferson, T. and Walker, M. (1993) 'Attitudes to the policing of ethnic minorities in a provincial city', *British Journal of Criminology*, 33(2): 251–66.

Jenkins, R. (1994) 'Rethinking ethnicity: identity, categorization and power', *Ethnic and Racial Studies*, 17(2): 197–223.

Jenkins, R. (1996) *Social Identity*. London: Routledge.

Jenkins, R. (1997) *Rethinking Ethnicity: Arguments and Explorations*. London: Sage.

Jenkins, R. (2000) 'Categorization: identity, social process, and epistemology', *Current Sociology*, 48(3): 7–25.

Jewkes, Y. (2004) *Media and Crime*. London: Sage.

Johnstone, J., Hawkins, D. and Michener, A (1994) 'Homicide reporting in Chicago dailies', *Journalism Quarterly*, 71(4): 860–72.

Khan, K. (1999) 'Race, drugs and prevalence', *International Journal of Drug Policy*, 10(2): 83–8.

Kidd-Hewitt, D. (1995) 'Crime and the media: a criminological perspective', in D. Kidd-Hewitt and R. Osborne (eds), *Crime and the Media: The Post-Modern Spectacle*. London: Pluto, pp. 1–24.

Kivivuori, J. (1998) 'Delinquent phases: the case of temporally intensified shoplifting behaviour', *British Journal of Criminology*, 38(4): 663–80.

Knight, T., Mowlam, A., Woodfield, W., Lewis, J., Purdon, S. and Kitchen, S. with Roberts, C. (2003) *Evaluation of the Community Sentences and Withdrawal of Benefits Pilot*, Research Report 198. Leeds: Corporate Document Services.

Korf, D., Bless, R. and Nottelman, N. (1998) *Urban Drug Problems and the General Public*. Lisbon: EMCDDA.

Kovach, B. and Rosenstiel, T. (2001) *The Elements of Journalism*. London: Atlantic Books.

Lahey, B. B. and Waldman, I. D. (2003) 'A developmental propensity model of the origins of conduct problems during childhood and adolescence', in B. B. Lahey,

T. E. Moffitt and A. Caspi (eds), *Causes of Conduct Disorder and Juvenile Delinquency*. New York: Guilford.

Lea, J. and Young, J. (1982) 'The riots in Britain 1981: urban violence and marginalisation', in D. Cowell, T. Jones and J. Young (eds), *Policing the Riots*. London: Junction Books, pp. 5–20.

Lea, J. and Young, J. (1984) *What Is To Be Done about Law and Order?* London: Penguin.

LeBlanc, M. (1997) 'A generic control theory of the criminal phenomenon: the structural and dynamic statements of an integrative multilayered control theory', in T. P. Thornberry (ed.), *Developmental Theories of Crime and Delinquency*, Advances in Criminological Theory, Vol. 7. New Brunswick, NJ: Transaction.

Lessig, L. (1999) *Code and Other Laws of Cyberspace*. New York: Basic Books.

Lévi-Strauss, C. (1975) *Mythologiques*, Vol. 1. New York: Charles Scribner's Sons.

Loeber, R. (1996) 'Developmental continuity, change, and pathway, in male juvenile problem behaviours and delinquency', in J. D. Hawkins (ed.), *Delinquency and Crime: Current Theories*. Cambridge: Cambridge University Press.

Lyng, S. (ed.) (2004) *Edgework: The Sociology of Risk-Taking*. New York and London: Routledge.

Lyon, D. (1994) *The Electronic Eye: The Rise of Surveillance Society*. Cambridge: Polity Press; Malden, MA: Blackwell.

Lyon, D. (1997) 'Cyberspace sociality: controversies over computer-mediated communication', in B. Loader (ed.), *The Governance of Cyberspace*. London and New York: Routledge, pp. 23–37.

Lyon, D. (2001a) *Surveillance Society: Monitoring Everyday Life*. Buckingham: Open University Press.

Lyon, D. (2001b) 'Facing the future: seeking ethics for everyday surveillance', *Information Technology and Ethics*, 1–10.

Lyon, D. (2003) *Surveillance after September 11*. Cambridge: Polity.

McCullagh, C. (2002) *Media Power: A Sociological Introduction*. Basingstoke: Palgrave.

Macfarlane, R. (2003) *Mountains of the Mind: A History of a Fascination*. London: Granta Books

McKeganey, N. (1998) 'Alcopops and young people: a suitable cause for concern', *Addiction*, 93: 471–3.

McKeganey, N., Forsyth, A., Barnard, M. and Hay, G. (1996) 'Designer drinks and drunkenness in a sample of Scottish schoolchildren', *British Medical Journal*, 313: 401.

Macpherson, Sir william (1999) *The Stephen Lawrence Inquiry*. London: Home Office.

Mannheim, H. (1965) *Comparative Criminology*. London: Routledge.

Manning, P. (1977) *Police Work*. Cambridge, MA: MIT Press.

Marsh, P. and Fox Kibby, K. (1992) *Drinking and Public Disorder: A Report of Research Conducted for The Portman Group by MCM Research*. London: Portman Group. Also available online.

Marvin, C. (1988) *When Old Technologies Were New*. Oxford and New York: Oxford University Press.

Massey, D. (1984) *Spatial Divisions of Labour. Social Structure and the Geography of Production*, 2nd edn. Basingstoke: Macmillan.

Matza, D. (1964) *Delinquency and Drift*. New York: Wiley.

Matza, D. (1969) *Becoming Deviant*. Englewood Cliffs, NJ: Prentice Hall.

May, T. and Hough, H. (2001) 'Illegal dealings: the impact of low-level police enforcement on drug markets', *European Journal on Criminal Policy and Research*, 9: 137–62.

May, T., Warburton, H., Turnbull, P. and Hough, M. (2002) *Times They Are A-changing: Policing of Cannabis*. York: Joseph Rowntree Foundation.

Mead, G. H. (1934) *Mind, Self and Society*. Chicago, IL: University of Chicago.

Mead, L. (1986) *Beyond Entitlement*. New York: Free Press.

Measham, F. (1996) 'The "Big Bang" approach to sessional drinking: changing patterns of alcohol consumption amongst young people in north west England', *Addiction Research*, 4(3): 283–99.

Measham, F. (2002) '"Doing gender" – "doing drugs": conceptualising the gendering of drugs cultures', *Contemporary Drug Problems*, 29(2): 335–73.

Measham, F. (2004a) 'The decline of ecstasy, the rise of "binge drinking" and the persistence of pleasure', *Probation Journal*, Special Edition: Rethinking Drugs and Crime, 51(4): 309–26.

Measham, F. (2004b) 'Play space: historical and socio-cultural reflections on drugs, licensed leisure locations, commercialisation and control', *International Journal of Drug Policy*, Special Edition: Social Theory in Drug Research and Harm Reduction, 15(5–6): 337–45.

Measham, F. (2004c) 'Drug and alcohol research: the case for cultural criminology', in J. Ferrell, K. Hayward, W. Morrison and M. Presdee (eds), *Cultural Criminology Unleashed*. London: Glasshouse, pp. 207–18.

Measham, F., Aldridge, J. and Parker, H. (2001) *Dancing on Drugs: Risk, Health and Hedonism in the British Club Scene*. London: Free Association Books.

Measham, F., Newcombe, R. and Parker, H. (1994) 'The normalization of recreational drug use amongst young people in North-West England', *British Journal of Sociology*, 45(2): 287–312.

Melucci, A. (1996) *Challenging Codes: Collective Action in the Information Age*. Cambridge, New York and Melbourne: Cambridge University Press.

Merton, R. (1938) 'Social structure and anomie', *American Sociological Review*, 3: 672–82.

Michael, J. and Adler, M. J. (1933) *Crime, Law and Social Science*. New York: Harcourt, Brace.

Miles, R. (1989) *Racism*. London: Routledge.

Miller, J., Bland, N. and Quinton, P. (2001) 'A challenge for police–community relations: rethinking stop and search in England and Wales', *European Journal on Criminal Policy and Research*, 9: 71–93.

Mills, C. W. (1959) *The Sociological Imagination*. New York: Oxford University Press.

Moffitt, T. E. (1993) 'Adolescence-limited and life-course-persistent antisocial behavior: a developmental taxonomy', *Psychological Review*, 100: 674–701.

Moore, K. and Miles, S. (2004) Young people, dance and the sub-cultural consumption of drugs, *Addiction Research and Theory*, 12(6): 507–23.

Morgan, P. (1995) *Farewell to the Family? Public Policy and Family Breakdown in Britain and the USA*. London: Institute of Economic Affairs.

Muncie, J. (2001) 'New criminology', in E. McLaughlin and J. Muncie (eds), *The Sage Dictionary of Criminology*. London: Sage, pp. 187–8.

Murji, K. (1999) 'White lines: culture, "race" and drugs', in N. South (ed.), *Drugs: Cultures, Controls and Everyday Life*. London: Sage, pp. 49–65.

Murray, C. (1984) *Losing Ground. American Social Policy 1950–1980*. New York: Basic Books.

Murray, C. (1990) *The Emerging British Underclass*. London: Institute of Economic Affairs Health and Welfare Unit.

Murray, C. (1994) *Underclass: The Crisis Deepens*. London: Institute of Economic Affairs Health and Welfare Unit.

Naffine, N. and Gale, F. (1989) 'Testing the nexus: crime, gender, and unemployment', *British Journal of Criminology*, 29(2):144–56.

National Fire Protection Association (2000) *U.S. Arson Trends and Patterns*. Quincy, MA: NFPA.

National Statistics (2003) *Share of the Wealth*. Online at: http://www.statistics.gov.uk/cci/nugget.asp?id=2 (accessed 17 June 2004).

Nelkin, D. (1995) 'Forms of intrusion: comparing resistance to information technology and biotechnology in America', in M. Bauer (ed.), *Resistance to New Technology*. Cambridge, New York and Melbourne: Cambridge University Press, pp. 379–90.

New York Times (2000) 'One consulting firm finds voter data is hot property', 9 September.

Newcombe, R. (1996) 'Live and let die: is methadone more likely to kill you than heroin?', *Druglink*, 11(1): 9–12.

Nicholls, C. S. (ed.) (1996) *The Hutchinson Encyclopaedia of Biography*. Oxford: Helicon.

Nock, S. L. (1993) *The Costs of Privacy: Surveillance and Reputation in America*. New York: Walter de Gruyter.

Norris, C. and Armstrong, G. (1999) *The Maximum Surveillance Society: The Rise of CCTV*. London: Berg.

Novak, T. (1988) *Poverty and the State. An Historical Sociology*. Buckingham: Open University Press.

Office of the Deputy Prime Minister (2003) *Arson Control Forum Annual Report*. London: Government Printers.

Office of the Deputy Prime Minister (2004a) (Draft) *Fire and Rescue National Framework*. London: Government Printers.

Office of the Deputy Prime Minister (2004b) *Arson Control Forum Annual Report*. London: Government Printers.

Office of the Deputy Prime Minister (2004c) *Arson Control Forum Statistics*. London: Government Printers.

Omi, M. and Winant, M. (1994) *Racial Formation in the United States*. London: Routledge.

Orford, J. (1985) *Excessive Appetites: A Psychological View of Addictions*. Chichester: Wiley.

Parker, H. (2001) 'Unbelievable? The UK's drugs present', in H. Parker, J. Aldridge and R. Egginton, *UK Drugs Unlimited: New Research and Policy Lessons on Illicit Drug Use*. Basingstoke: Palgrave, pp. 1–13.

Parker, H., Aldridge, J. and Measham, F. (1998) *Illegal Leisure: The Normalization of Adolescent Recreational Drug Use*. London: Routledge.

Parker, H., Bakx, K. and Newcombe, R. (1988) *Living with Heroin: The Impact of a Drugs 'Epidemic' on an English community*. Milton Keynes: Open University Press.

Parker, H., Williams, L. and Aldridge, J. (2002) 'The normalisation of "sensible" recreational drug use: further evidence from the north west England longitudinal study', *Sociology*, 36(4): 941–64.

Pasquino, P. (1991) 'Criminology: the birth of a special knowledge', in G. Burchell, C. Gordon and P. Miller (eds), *The Foucault Effect: Studies in Governmentality*. Hemel Hempstead: Harvester Wheatsheaf, pp. 235–50.

Pavis, S., Cunningham-Burley, S. and Amos, A. (1998) 'Health related behavioural change in context: young people in transition', *Social Science and Medicine*, 47(10): 1407–18.

Pawson, R. and Tilley, N. (1997) *Realistic Evaluation*. London: Sage.

Pearson, G. (1983) *Hooligan: A History of Respectable Fears*. Basingstoke: Macmillan.

Pearson, G. (2001) 'Normal drug use: ethnographic fieldwork among an adult network of recreational drug users in inner London', *Substance Use and Misuse*, 36(1): 167–99.

Pearson, G. and Shiner, M. (2002) 'Rethinking the generation gap: attitudes to illicit drugs among young people and adults', *Criminal Justice*, 2(1): 71–86.

Peele, S. and Grant, M. (eds) (1999) *Alcohol and Pleasure: A Health Perspective*. Philadelphia, PA: Brunner/Mazel.

Peelo, M. and Soothill, K. (2000) 'The place of public narratives in reproducing social order', *Theoretical Criminology*, 4(2): 131–48.

Peelo, M., Francis, B., Soothill, K. and Pearson, J. (2004) 'Newspaper reporting and the public construction of homicide', *British Journal of Criminology*, 44(2): 256–75.

Pfohl, S. (1994) *Images of Deviance and Social Control*. New York: McGraw-Hill.

Piachaud, D. and Sutherland, H. (2000) *How Effective is the British Government's Attempt to Reduce Child Poverty?*, CASE Paper 38. London: Centre for Analysis of Social Exclusion.

Plant, S. (1999) *Writing on Drugs*. London: Faber & Faber.

Police Foundation, (2000) *Drugs and the Law: Report of the Independent Inquiry into the Misuse of Drugs Act 1971*. London: Police Foundation.

Potter, W. J. (2003) *The 11 Myths of Media Violence*. Thousand Oaks, CA: Sage.

Presdee, M. (2000) *Cultural Criminology and the Carnival of Crime*. London: Routledge.

Presdee, M. (2004a) 'Cultural criminology: the long and winding road', *Theoretical Criminology*, 8(3): 275–85.

Presdee, M. (2004b) 'The story of crime: biography and the excavation of transgression', in J. Ferrell, K. Hayward, W. Morrison and M. Presdee (eds), *Cultural Criminology Unleashed*. London: Glasshouse, pp. 41–9.

Pyne, S. J. (1995) *World Fire: The Culture of Fire on Earth*. New York: Henry Holt & Co.

Rafter, N. (1997) 'Psychopathy and the evolution of criminological knowledge', *Theoretical Criminology*, 1(2): 235–59.

Ramsay, M. and Percy, A. (1996) *Drug Misuse Declared: Results of the 1994 British Crime Survey*. London: Home Office.

Ramsay, M., Baker, P., Goulden, C., Sharp, C. and Sondhi, A. (2001) *Drug Misuse Declared in 2000: Results from the British Crime Survey*, Home Office Research Study No. 224. London: Home Office Research, Development and Statistics Directorate.

Redhead, S. (ed.) (1993) *Rave Off: Politics and Deviance in Contemporary Youth Culture*. Aldershot: Avebury.

Regan, P. (1995) *Legislating Privacy: Technology, Surveillance, and Public Policy*. Chapel Hill, NC: University of North Carolina Press.

Reiner, R. (2002) 'Media made criminality: the representations of crime in the mass media', in M. Maguire, R. Morgan and R. Reiner (eds), *The Oxford Handbook of Criminology*, 3rd edn. Oxford: Oxford University Press, pp. 376–416.

Richardson, A. and Budd, T. (2003) *Alcohol, Crime and Disorder: A Study of Young Adults*, Home Office Research Study No. 263. London: Home Office.

Rock, P. (1998) *After Homicide: Practical and Political Responses to Bereavement*. Oxford: Clarendon Press.

Rose, N. (1999) *Powers of Freedom: Reframing Political Thought*. Cambridge, New York and Melbourne: Cambridge University Press.

Rosen, A. (2003) *The Transformation of British Life 1952–2000: A Social History*. Manchester: Manchester University Press.

Rowe, M. (2004) *Policing, Race and Racism*. Collumpton: Willan.

Rule, J. (1973) *Private Lives, Public Surveillance*. London: Allen Lane.

Sampson, R. J. and Laub, J. (1993) *Crime in the Making: Pathways and Turning Points Through Life*. Cambridge, MA: Harvard University Press.

Sanders, B. (2005) 'In the club: ecstasy use and supply in a London nightclub', *Sociology* (forthcoming).

Saunders, T., Stone, V. and Candy, S. (2001) *The Impact of the 26 Week Sanctioning Regime*, Employment Service Report 100. Sheffield: Employment Service.

Schechner, R. (1988) *Performance Theory*. London: Routledge.

Shapiro, H. (1999) 'Dances with drugs: pop music, drugs and youth culture', in N. South (ed.), *Drugs: Cultures, Controls and Everyday Life*. London: Sage, pp. 17–35.

Shiner, M. (2003) 'Out of harm's way? Illicit drug use, medicalization and the law', *British Journal of Criminology*, 43: 772–96.

Shiner, M. and Newburn, T. (1997) 'Definitely, maybe not? The normalisation of recreational drug use amongst young people', *Sociology*, 31(3): 511–29.

Simpson, M. (2003) 'The relationship between drug use and crime: a puzzle inside an enigma', *International Journal of Drug Policy*, 14: 307–19.

Singer, M. (2003) 'Reversing the hierarchy: rethinking multidisciplinarity in drug research', *International Journal of Drug Policy*, 14(1): 111–14.

Skolnick, J. (1966) *Justice Without Trial: Law Enforcement in a Democratic Society*. New York and London: Wiley.

Slevin, J. (2000) *The Internet and Society*. Cambridge: Polity Press.

Smith, D. (1986) *Police and People in London*. Aldershot: Gower.

Smith, D. J. (1997) 'Ethnic origins, crime and criminal justice in England and Wales', *Crime and Justice*, ed. M. Tonry. Chicago, IL: University of Chicago Press, 21: 101–82.

Smith, D. and Stewart, J. (1997) 'Probation and social exclusion', *Social Policy and Administration*, 31(5): 96–115.

Social Exclusion Unit (2000) *Young People. Report of Policy Action Team 12*. London: Social Exclusion Unit.

Soothill, K. and Pope, J. (1973) 'Arson: a twenty-year cohort study', *Medicine, Science and Law*, 13(2): 127–38.

Soothill, K. and Walby, S. (1991) *Sex Crime in the News*. London: Routledge.

Soothill, K., Ackerley, E. and Francis, B. (2004a) 'The criminal careers of arsonists', *Medicine Science and the Law*, 44(1): 27–40.

Soothill, K., Ackerley, E. and Francis, B. (2004) 'Profiles of crime recruitment – changing patterns over time', *British Journal of Criminology*, 44(3): 401–18.

Soothill, K., Peelo, M. and Taylor, C. (2002) *Making Sense of Criminology*. Cambridge: Polity Press.

Soothill, K., Peelo, M., Francis, B., Pearson, J. and Ackerley, E. (2002) 'Homicide and the media: identifying the top cases in the *Times*', *Howard Journal of Criminal Justice*, 41(5): 401–21.

Sorenson, S., Peterson Manz, J., Berk, R. (1998) 'News media coverage and the epidemiology of homicide', *American Journal of Public Health*, 88(10): 1510–14.

South, N. (ed.) (1999) *Drugs: Cultures, Controls and Everyday Life*. London: Sage.

Staples, W. G. (2000) *Everyday Surveillance: Vigilance and Visibility in Postmodern Life*. Lanham, MD: Rowman & Littlefield.

Stellin, S. (2000) 'Dot-com liquidations put consumer data in limbo', *The New York Times*, 4 December.

Stevens, P. and Willis, C. (1979) *Race, Crime and Arrests*. London: Home Office.

Stewart, G. and Stewart, J. (1993) *Social Circumstances of Younger Offenders Under Supervision*. London: Association of Chief Officers of Probation.

Stimson, G. (2001) '"Blair declares war": the unhealthy state of British drug policy', *International Journal of Drug Policy*, 11(4): 259–64.

Strang, J. and Gossop, M. (eds) (1994) *Heroin and Drug Policy: The British System*. Oxford: Oxford University Press.

Strange, S. (1996) *The Retreat of the State: The Diffusion of Power in the World Economy*. Cambridge, New York and Melbourne: Cambridge University Press.

Strategy Unit (2004) *Alcohol Harm Reduction Strategy for England*. London: Cabinet Office, Prime Minister's Strategy Unit.

Suchman, L. (1994) 'Do categories have politics? The language/interaction perspective reconsidered', *Computer-Supported Cooperative Work*, 2: 177–90.

Sumner, M. and Parker, H. (1995) *Low in Alcohol: A Review of International Research into Alcohol's Role in Crime Causation*. London: Portman.

Sydney-Smith, S. (2002) *Beyond Dixon of Dock Green: Early British Police Series*. London: I.B. Taurus.

Taylor, I. (1999) *Crime in Context: A Critical Criminology of Market Societies*. Cambridge: Polity Press.

Taylor I., Walton, P. and Young, J. (1973) *The New Criminology*. London: Routledge & Kegan Paul.

Thompson, J. (1995) *The Media and Modernity*. Cambridge: Polity Press.

Thompson, K. (1998) *Moral Panics*. London: Routledge.

Thornberry, T. P. and Krohn, M. D. (2001) 'The development of delinquency: an interactional perspective', in S. O. White (ed.), *Handbook of Youth and Justice*. New York: Plenum.

Thornett, A. (1998) *Inside Cowley. Trade Union Struggle in the 1970s: Who Really opened the Door to the Tory Onslaught?* London: Porcupine Press.

Tonry, M. (ed.) (1997) *Ethnicity, Crime and Immigration. Comparative and Cross-National Perspectives*. Chicago and London: University of Chicago Press.

Torpey, J. (2000) *The Invention of the Passport: Surveillance, Citizenship, and the State*. Cambridge, New York and Melbourne: Cambridge University Press.

Travis, A. (2000) 'Police force urges legalisation', *Guardian*, 17 February.

Tremlett, G. (2003) 'Best case scenario for Spanish smokers', *Guardian*, 1 October.

Updated Drug Strategy (2002) London: Home Office.

US Fire Administration (2004) *Fire Data*. Washington: Department of Homeland Security.

Utting, D. (1995) *Family and Parenthood: Supporting Families and Preventing Breakdown*, Social Policy Summary 4. York: Joseph Rowntree Foundation. Online at: http://www.jrf.org.uk/knowledge/findings/socialpolicy/sp4.asp (accessed 21 July 2003).

Verma, S. (1999) 'Police double crime "hot-spot" targets', *Toronto Star*, 23 July, A1, A21.

Viano, M. (2002) 'An intoxicated screen: reflections on film and drugs', in J. Farrell Brodie and M. Redfield (eds), *High Anxieties: Cultural Studies in Addiction*. Berkeley, CA: University of California, pp. 134–58.

Virilio, P. (1997) 'The over-exposed city', in N. Leach (ed.), *Rethinking Architecture*. London and New York: Routledge.

Waddington, P. A. J., Stenson, K. and Don, D. (2004) 'In proportion: race, and police stop and search', *British Journal of Criminology*, 44(6): 889–914.

Walker, R. and Ahmad, W. (1994) 'Windows of opportunity in a rotting frame', *Critical Social Policy*, 40: 46–69.

Walklate, S. (1998) *Understanding Criminology: Current Theoretical Debates*. Buckingham: Open University Press.

Washington Post (2000) 'Internet users seek assurances over on-line use of personal data', 20 August. Online at: http://washingtonpost.com/wp-dyn/articles/A60984-2000Aug20.html

Weisner, M., Capaldi, D. M. and Patterson, G. R. (2003) 'Development of antisocial behavior and crime across the life-span from a social interactional perspective: The coercion model', in R. L. Akers and G. F. Jensen (eds). *Social Learning Theory and the Explanation of Crime*, Advances in Criminological Theory, Vol. 11. New Brunswick, NJ: Transaction.

West, D. and Farrington, D. (1973) *Who Becomes Delinquent?* London: Heinemann.

West, D. and Farrington, D. (1977) *The Delinquent Way of Life*. London: Heinemann.

Whittington, L., and Harper, T. (2001) 'Ottawa to boost terror laws', *Toronto Star*, 23 November, A1.

Wikström, P.-O. H. (1995) 'Self-control, temptations, frictions and punishment: An integrated approach to crime prevention', in P.-O. H. Wikström, R. V. Clarke and J. McCord (eds), *Integrating Crime Prevention Strategies: Propensity and Opportunity*. Stockholm: National Council for Crime Prevention.

Willott, S. and Griffin, C. (1999) 'Building your own lifeboat: working-class male offenders talk about economic crime', *British Journal of Social Psychology*, 38(4): 445–60.

Witt, R., Clarke, A. and Fielding, N. (1998) 'Crime, earnings and unemployment in England and Wales', *Applied Economic Letters*, 5(4): 265–7.

Young, J. (2003) 'Merton with energy, Katz with structure: the sociology of vindictiveness and the criminology of transgression', *Theoretical Criminology*, 7(3): 389–414.

Index

9/11 22
    effect on attitude to surveillance
        121, 134
    effect on police deployment in
        London 110
academic knowledge 136–7
ACPO (Association of Chief Police
    Officers) 43, 50, 51
acquisitive crime, relationship with
    drug use 94–5
actuality of crime x
    distancing from 31
'actuarial justice' 120–1
addiction 94
age effects xiv, 113, 114, 118
    for burglars 118
    and conviction rates 117
age-crime curve 114
'age-period interactions' 117
age-period-cohort studies 103–4
    analysis 115–18
    failing to take into account 115
    see also cohort effects; period effects
aggression and media representations
    of crime 31

alcohol 83, 96
    association between crime and 96
    changes in attitude towards 90
alcohol-related disorder 96
    responses 96–8
analysis of data *see* data analysis
'Anglicanised communitarianism' 64
anomie 10, 67
antisocial behaviour 64
    legislation for 81
application of criminology 139
applied social science studies x
    criminology as x–xi
arson xiii, 136
    cultural analysis of the causes or
        genesis 71
    as social edgework 79
    as the 'sublime' crime 80
Asians and the use of stop and search
    46, 88
Association of Chief Police Officers
    (ACPO) 43, 50, 51

behaviour, association between culture
    and 40